Japanese Cooking
made simple

Japanese Cooking
made simple

over 90 stylish recipes

yasuko fukuoka

southwater

This edition is published by Southwater, an imprint of Anness Publishing Ltd,
108 Great Russell Street, London WC1B 3NA; info@anness.com

www.southwaterbooks.com; www.annesspublishing.com; twitter: @Anness_Books

If you like the images in this book and would like to investigate using them for publishing, promotions
or advertising, please visit our website www.practicalpictures.com for more information.

© Anness Publishing Ltd 2015

Publisher: Joanna Lorenz
Editor: Clare Gooden
Photographer: Craig Robertson
Stylist: Helen Trent
Introduction by: Emi Kazuko
Designer: Nigel Partridge
Production Controller: Rosanna Anness

NOTES
Bracketed terms are intended for American readers.
For all recipes, quantities are given in both metric and imperial measures and,
where appropriate, in standard cups and spoons.
Follow one set of measures, but not a mixture, because they are not interchangeable.
Standard spoon and cup measures are level. 1 tsp = 5ml, 1 tbsp = 15ml, 1 cup = 250ml/8fl oz.
Australian standard tablespoons are 20ml. Australian readers should use 3 tsp in place of 1 tbsp for measuring small quantities.
American pints are 16fl oz/2 cups. American readers should use 20fl oz/2.5 cups in place of 1 pint when measuring liquids.
Electric oven temperatures in this book are for conventional ovens. When using a fan oven, the temperature will
probably need to be reduced by about 10–20°C/20–40°F. Since ovens vary, you should check with
your manufacturer's instruction book for guidance.
Medium (US large) eggs are used unless otherwise stated.

To avoid repetition, the method for making *su-meshi* and the instructions for
cooking rice are provided in full only the first time they appear in the recipe section:
on pages 12 and 20 respectively. For all later uses, refer to these pages.
The glossary at the back of the book provides a quick guide to unusual Japanese ingredients.

Front cover shows Tempura Seafood – for recipe, see page 96.

PUBLISHER'S NOTE
Although the advice and information in this book are believed to be accurate and true at the time of going
to press, neither the authors nor the publisher can accept any legal responsibility or liability for any errors or
omissions that may have been made nor for any inaccuracies nor for any loss, harm or injury that comes
about from following instructions or advice in this book.

CONTENTS

INTRODUCTION 6

SUSHI AND RICE 10

SOUPS AND NOODLES 28

VEGETABLES AND SEAWEED 42

BEANS, TOFU AND EGGS 66

FISH AND SHELLFISH 76

POULTRY AND MEAT 100

DESSERTS AND CAKES 114

GLOSSARY 122

SHOPPING INFORMATION 124

INDEX 126

INTRODUCTION

To many people, Japan is an exciting and exotic country, mixing tradition and modernity to striking effect. Its food culture is certainly no exception, and in many ways reflects Japanese culture. For example, the minimalism that exists in Japanese aesthetics, such as poetry and music, art and architecture, is also evident in the culinary culture, whether it be in the taste, flavour, presentation or in the cooking itself. Similarly, the meticulous attention to detail that the Japanese display in many areas, from painting to microchip production, is equally evident in their approach to food and drink.

FRESHNESS AND SIMPLICITY

Perhaps one of the defining features of the Japanese cuisine is the relationship that exists between how food is used and nature. Where possible, food is eaten in as natural a state as possible, as this is considered the best, if not the only, way to experience the true taste of food. This is at the heart of the Japanese philosophy of eating. So the fish and shellfish caught in the seas of Japan are often eaten raw, or only very lightly cured with vinegar or salt.

The simplicity and minimalism that underlie Japanese architecture and art are also reflected in their cuisine.

Likewise, fresh, seasonal agricultural products are only lightly cooked to preserve their bite and flavour, or they may be slightly salted. How and what people cook is also highly influenced by the season and by local produce. As a result, Japan is home to many delicious regional dishes.

To further maintain the purity of food, Japanese cooking rarely mixes different food types, and sauces are normally served in separate dishes as dipping condiments. This is in contrast to the practices of many other cuisines, which use long, slow cooking techniques, often with the addition of sauces and spices, so that the food becomes something that is very different from the raw ingredients.

RICE: A STAPLE FOOD FOR ALL

In Japan, rice is so important that the word for cooked rice, *gohan* or *meshi*, also means meal. Rice was probably introduced to Japan from South-east Asia – early steaming utensils have

been found, and there is evidence of rice having been boiled, steamed, grilled (broiled) and roasted in Japan as far back as 200BC.

People began to use rice as their basic daily food source because of its good storage qualities, rather than being dependent on less predictable crops, meats or fish and shellfish. It quickly became the staple food of Japan and the country's cuisine developed around it.

The production of rice is a communal process and villages became large rice production lines, cultivating the same land, generation after generation, for hundreds of years. The nation was founded on the basis of this village society and even in modern, highly industrialized Japan, this social cohesion is still evident.

With the development of rice cultivation, salt started to play a great part in the culinary scene. It was added to scarce animal or plant fibres and proteins to improve their storage qualities. This mixture, called hishio, was a nutritious fermented food as well as a seasoning, and was to become one of the most important developments in Japan's culinary history.

Five ingredients rice: one of many ways to enjoy Japan's staple ingredient.

Hishio later developed into some of the most well-known and important Japanese foods, such as miso and shoyu (grain hishio), shiokara and sushi (meat hishio), and tsukemono pickles (grass hishio).

The idea of fermentation was further developed to produce alcohol using barley, yam and glutinous rice. Although at first this was an alcoholic food, rather than a liquid, it was the origin of Japan's most celebrated drink, sake.

FOREIGN INFLUENCES

From the earliest times, neighbouring China and Korea have exerted great influence over Japan.

Japanese cooking is largely fish- and vegetable-based and if meat is included it is used very sparingly and often cooked with vegetables. This can be traced back to as early as the 6th century, when Buddhism first arrived via China, proclaiming animal slaughter and meat-eating to be sinful acts.

At the end of the 12th century, Zen, a strict sect of Buddhism, arrived from China and, with it, *shojin ryori*. This was originally simple vegan food cooked by the monks as part of their severe training. It usually consisted of a bowl of rice, soup and one or two other dishes, but it now refers to a formal vegetarian meal. Many Japanese dishes may appear to be vegetarian, however, vegetables are often cooked in dashi soup, which is a fish stock. Authentic *shojin ryori* should be purely vegan cooking.

Accompanying the Zen philosophical movement, Chinese foods and cooking techniques (particularly frying) were introduced to Japan. One important arrival was tea, which, although it had been brought back by earlier missions to China, did not become established as a drink among Buddhists and the upper classes until a Zen Buddhist brought back tea plant seeds at the end of the 12th century. This led eventually to the development of *cha-kaiseki* (the formal meal served before the tea ceremony), which established the form of Japanese cuisine.

EUROPEAN TRADE

Other foreigners, including the Spanish, Portuguese, Dutch and English, also greatly influenced Japan as trading with them progressed from the mid-16th century to the closure of the country in the early 17th century. These early foreigners, especially the Portuguese and Spanish, were disparagingly called *Nanban* (southern barbarians), because they arrived in Japan from the south through South-east Asia, and, to Japanese eyes, lacked sensitivity and bodily cleanliness.

The influence that their food and cooking methods had upon the Japanese cuisine is still evident today. Any dish or sauce with the name *Nanban* derives from this period; *nanban-zuke* (fried fish or vegetables marinated in a piquant, vinegary sauce) is one such dish. The name was also used to describe many other things, including paintings and furniture design.

With trade, many new vegetables and fruits also arrived: watermelons, sugar cane, chillies, figs, potatoes and the kabocha squash, which derives its name from its parent country, Cambodia. The Portuguese also brought the tomato to Japan, although initially only as a decorative plant.

The most famous foreign import of this period, tempura, was introduced by the Portuguese Jesuits and is now one of the most popular Japanese dishes. The first Tokugawa shogun, Ieyasu, liked sea-bream tempura so much that he died from overeating it!

Meat-eating was eventually reintroduced by the *Nanban* and became popular among Catholic feudal lords. Red wine and shochu (spirit distilled from sake) also appeared at this time and were seen as *Nanban* drinks.

Tempura was brought to Japan by the Portuguese Jesuits and remains among the most popular Japanese dishes.

Meat was reintroduced to Japan in the mid-19th century, when dishes such as sukiyaki *were invented.*

THE IMPACT OF ISOLATION

The closure of Japan to outside contact for 260 years, from the early 17th century, gave *washoku* (Japanese food) an opportunity to establish its own unique identity.

Tokyo became a centre where foods and cooking techniques converged. The regional lords were required to visit Tokyo in turn, bringing their local produce with them. This constant arrival of new ingredients and cooking methods contributed to the rich and varied character of Japanese cuisine.

After the country was opened up in the mid-19th century, meat-eating was reintroduced. The emperor Meiji Tenno himself ate beef in 1872 and this convinced the public that meat-eating was something new and fashionable. Beef-based dishes, such as *sukiyaki* and *shabu shabu*, are inventions of this period. French and English breads also flooded in, but they were regarded as snacks and cakes.

European cooking methods and ingredients were integrated into Japanese cooking, and many eclectic dishes, called *yōshoku* (Western food) as opposed to *washoku*, were created. *Tonkatsu*, pork cutlet, is the most noteworthy, and numerous *tonkatsu* restaurants opened up all over Japan.

SUSHI: A NATIONAL FAVOURITE

No one really knows when the word sushi was first used; strictly, it means to vinegar (originally the rice was thrown away), but as the vinegared rice became the essential ingredient, sushi developed into a term signifying vinegared rice dishes. The most famous sushi, *nigiri*, are hand-moulded fingers of vinegared rice with raw fish on top.

Today, sushi restaurants abound and sushi chefs are regarded as highly skilled craftsmen who must train for a number of years. Indeed, top sushi restaurants are very expensive. Even though sushi remains a snack food, it is undoubtedly a high-quality one.

THE TEA CEREMONY

If it was the English who transformed tea drinking into a lifestyle, it was the Japanese who perfected it as an art form. The tea ceremony is the essence of Japanese culture itself, embracing all divisions of visual art such as scrolled paintings and calligraphy, pottery, flower arranging and even architecture. The tea ceremony expresses the Japanese philosophy of life and etiquette, not just for drinking tea but for entertaining guests and being entertained. It teaches a person where they stand in society and how to behave.

At about the same time as the tea ceremony was being developed, a form of *shojin ryori* (the Zen Buddhist monks' vegetarian cooking) was brought back from China. *Cha-kaiseki*, the formal meal served before the tea ceremony, was developed in line with *shojin ryori*, and consisted of bowls of rice and soup with only two or three other dishes.

Present-day *cha-kaiseki* consists of up to 12 dishes, depending on the occasion, often accompanied by sake. The tea ceremony preceded by *cha-kaiseki* is known as *chaji* and the dishes should reflect the season in which the *chaji* is held.

Sushi is a national favourite in Japan and its appeal has spread worldwide.

SEASONAL AND REGIONAL FOODS

The seasons in Japan last for about three months each, with each new season bringing different produce and a changing catch of fish from the surrounding seas. In Japanese cooking, the idea of season persists strongly. There is even a word for seasonal food, *shun*, and locals will always look out for something that is in *shun*.

Geographically, Japan stretches through 16 degrees of latitude, from the northernmost island, alongside Russia, to the southern extreme near to South Korea, with local produce varying from region to region. Japan is also a country with huge mountain ranges running through the centre from north to south, covering some 75–80 per cent of the land. As a result, the produce varies not only by season and region but also by altitude.

The clash of warm and cold currents makes the seas around Japan among the world's richest fisheries, with an enormously varied range of fish and shellfish. Japan consumes some 3000 different kinds daily, and that total does not include regional varieties.

The regional foods and dishes in Japan vary greatly from Hokkaido, the northern island, to Kyushu, the southern island. Local restaurants are the best places to taste regional variations, though all local cuisines are represented in Tokyo and Osaka. The regions are so proud and eager to promote their speciality foods that they even produce their own versions of *bento* (packed lunch) using local produce, which are sold on the platforms of their mainline stations.

ALCOHOLIC DRINKS

There have been many attempts in the West to find out which wine goes best with Japanese food, but nothing really matches the mellow, delicate flavour of sake because it does not override the subtle nature of Japanese cuisine. While wine may have been developed to complement food, it was the other way round with sake. It is no exaggeration to claim that Japanese cuisine was developed together with, perhaps even for tasting with, sake.

The Japanese drink lager beer more than any other alcoholic beverage and often start a meal with a glass of ice-cold lager. The lager is usually followed by sake, which is drunk cold in summer and warm in winter, or by shochu (sake spirit), a very alcoholic beverage. One of the more popular ways of drinking shochu is to dilute it with hot water and add an umeboshi (dried salted Japanese apricot) to it.

PREPARATION AND COOKING METHODS

As dishes are often served raw or only lightly cooked, careful selection of ingredients is one of the most important aspects of Japanese cooking, and is also where a real part of the pleasure resides.

As the food is eaten with hashi (chopsticks), it needs to be cut into bitesize pieces. Vegetables are best eaten raw but they may be very lightly cooked; fresh fish is almost always filleted and often thinly sliced to eat raw as *sashimi*; and meat is usually thinly sliced or minced (ground).

Japan stretches through 16 degrees of latitude and local produce varies accordingly. Extensive mountain ranges and the surrounding seas further add to the variety of produce found in any one area.

Cooking methods include simmering, grilling (broiling), steaming and frying. Many fish and vegetable dishes involve griddling over a direct heat, in which case pan-frying may be substituted. Japanese cooking also uses various pickling and marinating methods.

No special knowledge is needed to create the following recipes and, apart from a few absolute essentials, such as a pair of chopsticks, most kitchens will easily be able to accommodate Japanese recipes with minimal fuss.

The recipes offer the best of local and national Japanese cuisine, from simple sushi appetizers to hotpots for all to share. As they say in Japan, just heed what nature is offering and enjoy.

SUSHI AND RICE

Rice is the very essence of Japanese cooking. Almost every

dish in Japanese cuisine is designed to accompany a bowl of

carefully prepared rice, not the other way round. This

chapter explains how to cook Japanese short grain rice to eat

by itself, and how to "vinegar" it for sushi. It also contains

some nutritious rice dishes, which are a meal in themselves.

MARINATED MACKEREL SUSHI

FRESH MACKEREL FILLETS ARE MARINATED, THEN PACKED INTO A MOULD WITH SUSHI RICE TO MAKE SABA-ZUSHI. START PREPARATIONS 8 HOURS IN ADVANCE TO ALLOW THE FISH TO ABSORB THE SALT.

MAKES ABOUT TWELVE

INGREDIENTS
500g/1¼lb mackerel, filleted
salt
rice vinegar
2cm/¾in fresh root ginger, peeled and
    finely grated, to garnish
shoyu, to serve
For the *su-meshi* (vinegared rice)
200g/7oz/1 cup Japanese short
    grain rice
40ml/8 tsp rice vinegar
20ml/4 tsp caster (superfine) sugar
5ml/1 tsp salt

1 Place the fillets skin side down in a flat dish, cover with a thick layer of salt, and leave them for 3–5 hours.

2 To make the *su-meshi*, put the rice in a large bowl and wash in plenty of water, until it runs clear. Tip into a sieve and leave to drain for 1 hour.

3 Put the rice into a small, deep pan with 15 per cent more water, i.e. 250ml/ 8fl oz/1⅛ cups water to 200g/7oz/1 cup rice. Cover and bring to the boil. This takes about 5 minutes. Reduce the heat and simmer for 12 minutes without lifting the lid. You should hear a faint crackling noise. The rice should now have absorbed the water. Remove from the heat and leave for 10 minutes.

4 Transfer the cooked rice to a wet Japanese rice tub or large bowl. In a small bowl, mix the vinegar, sugar and salt until well dissolved. Add to the rice, fluffing the rice with a wet spatula. Do not mash. If you have someone to help you, ask them to fan the rice to cool it quickly. This process makes the *su-meshi* glossy. Cover the bowl with wet dishtowels and leave to cool.

COOK'S TIP
All future uses, or variations, of *su-meshi* are based on the basic recipe provided above, hereafter referred to as 1 quantity of *su-meshi*.

5 Wipe the salt from the mackerel with kitchen paper. Remove all the remaining bones with tweezers. Lift the skin at the tail end of each fillet and peel towards the head end. Place the skinned fillets in a clean dish, and pour in enough rice vinegar to cover the fish completely. Leave for 20 minutes, then drain and wipe dry with kitchen paper.

6 Line a 25 × 7.5 × 4cm/10 × 3 × 1½in container with some clear film (plastic wrap), twice the size of the container. Lay the fillets in the container, skinned side down, to cover the base. Cut the remaining mackerel to fill the gaps.

7 Put the *su-meshi* into the container, and press down firmly with dampened hands. Cover with the clear film and place a weight on top. Leave for at least 3 hours or overnight.

8 Remove the sushi from its container, then slice into 2cm/¾in pieces. After each slice, wipe the knife with kitchen paper dampened with rice vinegar.

9 Arrange on a plate and add a little grated ginger. Serve with shoyu.

HAND-MOULDED SUSHI

ORIGINALLY DEVELOPED IN TOKYO AS STREET FINGER FOOD, NIGIRI-ZUSHI IS PREPARED WITH THE FRESHEST OF FISH AND EATEN WITHIN A MATTER OF A FEW MINUTES OF MAKING.

SERVES FOUR

INGREDIENTS
  4 raw king prawns (jumbo shrimp), head and shell removed, tails intact
  4 scallops, white muscle only
  425g/15oz assorted fresh seafood, skinned, cleaned and filleted
  2 quantities *su-meshi*
  15ml/1 tbsp rice vinegar, for moulding
  45ml/3 tbsp wasabi paste from a tube, or the same amount of wasabi powder mixed with 15ml/1 tbsp water
  salt
  gari, to garnish
  shoyu, to serve

1 Insert a bamboo skewer or cocktail stick (toothpick) into each prawn lengthways. This stops the prawns curling up when cooked. Boil them in lightly salted water for 2 minutes, or until they turn pink. Drain and cool, then pull out the skewers. Cut open from the belly side but do not slice in two. With the point of a sharp knife, scoop up the black vein running down its length. Very gently pull it out, then discard. Open out flat and place on a tray.

2 Slice the scallops horizontally in half, but not quite through. Gently open each scallop at this "hinge" to make a butterfly shape. Place on the tray, cut-side down. Use a sharp knife to cut all the fish fillets into 7.5 × 4cm/3 × 1½in pieces, 5mm/¼in thick. Place all the raw fish and shellfish on the tray, cover with clear film (plastic wrap), then chill.

3 Place the *su-meshi* in a bowl. Have ready a small bowl filled with 150ml/¼ pint/⅔ cup water and the vinegar for moulding. This water is used for your hands while making *nigiri-zushi*. Take the tray of toppings from the refrigerator.

COOK'S TIP
Don't worry if your *su-meshi* block doesn't look very neat. Wet your hands with the hand water frequently, and keep the work surface tidy at all times.

4 Wet your hand with the vinegared water and scoop about 25ml/1½ tbsp *su-meshi* into your palm. Gently but firmly grip the *su-meshi* and make a rectangular block. Do not squash the rice, but ensure that the grains stick together. The size of the blocks must be smaller than the toppings.

5 Put the *su-meshi* block on a damp chopping board. Taking a piece of topping in your palm, rub a little wasabi paste in the middle of it. Put the *su-meshi* block on top of the fish slice and gently press it. Form your palm into a cup and shape the *nigiri-zushi* to a smooth-surfaced mound. Place it on a serving tray. Do not overwork, as the warmth of your hands can cause the toppings to lose their freshness.

6 Repeat this process until all of the rice and toppings are used. Serve immediately with a little shoyu dribbled on individual plates. To eat, pick up one *nigiri-zushi* and dip the tip into the shoyu. Eat a little gari between tasting different sushi to refresh your mouth.

JEWEL-BOX SUSHI

CHIRASHI IS THE MOST COMMON FORM OF SUSHI EATEN AT HOME IN JAPAN. A LACQUERED CONTAINER IS FILLED WITH SU-MESHI, AND VARIOUS COLOURFUL TOPPINGS ARE ARRANGED ON TOP.

SERVES FOUR

INGREDIENTS
2 eggs, beaten
vegetable oil, for frying
50g/2oz mangetouts
  (snow peas), trimmed
1 nori sheet
15ml/1 tbsp shoyu
15ml/1 tbsp wasabi paste from a
  tube, or the same amount of wasabi
  powder mixed with 10ml/2 tsp water
1¼ quantity *su-meshi* made with
  40ml/8 tsp sugar
salt
30–60ml/2–4 tbsp ikura, to garnish
For the fish and shellfish toppings
  115g/4oz very fresh tuna steak,
    skin removed
  90g/3½oz fresh squid, body only,
    cleaned and boned
  4 raw king prawns (jumbo shrimp),
    heads and shells removed,
    tails intact
For the shiitake
  8 dried shiitake mushrooms, soaked
    in 350ml/12fl oz/1½ cups water for
    4 hours
  15ml/1 tbsp caster (superfine) sugar
  60ml/4 tbsp mirin
  45ml/3 tbsp shoyu

1 Slice the tuna across the grain into 7.5 × 4cm/3 × 1½in pieces, 5mm/¼in thick, using a very sharp knife. Slice the squid crossways into 5mm/¼in strips. Place both on a tray, cover with clear film (plastic wrap) and chill.

2 Remove and discard the stalks from the shiitake. Pour the soaking water into a pan, add the shiitake and bring to the boil. Skim the surface and reduce the heat. Cook for 20 minutes, then add the sugar. Reduce the heat further and add the mirin and shoyu. Simmer until almost all the liquid has evaporated. Drain and slice very thinly. Set aside.

3 Insert a bamboo skewer into each prawn lengthways. Boil in salted water for 2 minutes. Drain and leave to cool.

4 Remove the skewers from the prawns. Cut open from the belly side but do not slice in two. Remove the black vein. Open out flat and add to the tray.

5 Beat the eggs in a mixing bowl and add a pinch of salt. Heat a little oil in a frying pan until it smokes. Wipe away the excess oil with kitchen paper. Add enough beaten egg to thinly cover the bottom of the frying pan while tilting the pan. Cook on a medium low heat until the edge is dry and starting to curl. Lift the omelette and turn over. After 30 seconds, transfer to a chopping board. Use the remaining egg mixture to make several omelettes. Pile them up and roll them together into a tube. Slice very thinly to make strands.

6 Par-boil the mangetouts for 2 minutes in lightly salted water, then drain. Cut into 3mm/⅛in diagonal strips. Snip the nori into fine shreds using scissors. Mix with the shoyu and wasabi.

7 Divide half the *su-meshi* among four large rice bowls. Spread a quarter of the nori mixture over each bowl of *su-meshi*. Cover with the rest of the *su-meshi*. Flatten the surface with a wet spatula.

8 Sprinkle over egg strands to cover the surface completely. Arrange the tuna slices in a fan shape with a fan of shiitake on top. Place a prawn next to the tuna, and arrange the squid strips in a heap on the other side. Arrange the mangetouts and ikura decoratively on top.

HAND-ROLLED SUSHI

THIS IS A FUN WAY TO ENJOY SUSHI. CALLED TEMAKI-ZUSHI, *MEANING HAND-ROLLED, EACH GUEST ROLLS TOGETHER INDIVIDUAL FILLINGS OF FISH AND SHELLFISH, VEGETABLES AND* SU-MESHI.

SERVES FOUR TO SIX

INGREDIENTS
    2 quantities *su-meshi*, made with
        40ml/8 tsp caster (superfine) sugar
    225g/8oz extremely fresh tuna steak
    130g/4½oz smoked salmon
    17cm/6½in Japanese cucumber or
        salad cucumber
    8 raw king prawns (jumbo shrimp)
        or large tiger prawns, peeled and
        heads removed
    1 avocado
    7.5ml/1½ tsp lemon juice
    20 chives, trimmed and chopped into
        6cm/2½in lengths
    1 packet mustard and cress, roots
        cut off
    6–8 shiso leaves, cut in
        half lengthways
To serve
    12 nori sheets, cut into four
    mayonnaise
    shoyu
    45ml/3 tbsp wasabi paste from a
        tube, or the same amount of
        wasabi powder mixed with 15ml/
        1 tbsp water
    gari

1 Put the *su-meshi* into a large serving bowl and cover with a damp dishtowel.

2 Slice the tuna, with the grain, into 5mm/¼in slices then into 1 x 6cm/½ x 2½in strips. Cut the salmon and cucumber into strips the same size as the tuna.

3 Insert bamboo skewers into the prawns, then boil in lightly salted water for 2 minutes. Drain and leave to cool. Remove the skewers and cut in half lengthways. Remove the vein.

4 Halve the avocado and remove the stone (pit). Sprinkle with half the lemon juice and cut into 1cm/½in long strips. Sprinkle on the remaining lemon juice.

5 Arrange the fish, shellfish, avocado and vegetables on a plate. Place the nori sheets on a few plates and put the mayonnaise into a bowl. Put the shoyu in individual bowls, and the wasabi paste in a dish. Heap the gari in a small bowl. Half-fill a glass with water and place four to six rice paddles inside. Arrange everything on the table.

6 Each guest rolls their sushi as follows: take a sheet of nori on your palm, then scoop out 45ml/3 tbsp rice and spread it on the nori sheet. Spread some wasabi in the middle of the rice, then place a few strips of different fillings on top. Roll it up as a cone and dip the end into the shoyu. Have some gari between rolls to refresh your mouth.

NORI-ROLLED SUSHI

YOU WILL NEED A MAKISU (A SUSHI ROLLING MAT) TO MAKE THESE SUSHI, CALLED NORI MAKI. THERE ARE TWO TYPES: HOSO-MAKI (THIN-ROLLED SUSHI) AND FUTO-MAKI (THICK-ROLLED SUSHI).

SERVES SIX TO EIGHT

FUTO-MAKI (THICK-ROLLED SUSHI)
MAKES SIXTEEN PIECES

INGREDIENTS
   2 nori sheets
   1 quantity *su-meshi*
For the omelette
   2 eggs, beaten
   25ml/1½ tbsp second dashi stock,
      or the same amount of water and
      5ml/1 tsp dashi-no-moto
   10ml/2 tsp sake
   2.5ml/½ tsp salt
   vegetable oil, for frying
For the fillings
   4 dried shiitake mushrooms, soaked
      in a bowl of water overnight
   120ml/4fl oz/½ cup second dashi
      stock, or the same amount of water
      and 1½ tsp dashi-no-moto
   15ml/1 tbsp shoyu
   7.5ml/1½ tsp caster (superfine) sugar
   5ml/1 tsp mirin
   6 raw large prawns (shrimp), heads
      and shells removed, tails intact
   4 asparagus spears, boiled for
      1 minute in lightly salted
      water, cooled
   10 chives, about 23cm/9in long,
      ends trimmed

1 To make the omelette, mix the beaten eggs, dashi stock, sake and salt in a bowl. Heat a little oil in a frying pan on a medium-low heat. Pour in just enough egg mixture to thinly cover the base of the pan. As soon as the mixture sets, fold the omelette in half towards you and wipe the space left with a little oil.

2 With the first omelette still in the pan, repeat this process of frying and folding to make more omelettes. Each new one is laid on to the previous omelette, to form one multi-layered omelette. When all the mixture is used, slide the layered omelette on to a chopping board. Cool, then cut into 1cm/½in wide strips.

3 Put the shiitake, dashi stock, shoyu, sugar and mirin in a small pan. Bring to the boil then reduce the heat to low. Cook for 20 minutes until half of the liquid has evaporated. Drain, remove and discard the stalks, and slice the caps thinly. Squeeze out any excess liquid, then dry on kitchen paper.

4 Make three cuts in the belly of the prawns to stop them curling up, and boil in salted water for 1 minute, or until they turn bright pink. Drain and cool, then remove the vein.

5 Place a nori sheet at the front edge of the makisu. Scoop up half of the *su-meshi* and spread it on the nori as in *hoso-maki*. Leave a 1cm/½in margin at the side nearest you, and 2cm/¾in at the side furthest from you.

6 Make a shallow depression horizontally across the centre of the rice. Fill this with a row of omelette strips, then put half the asparagus and prawns on top. Place 5 chives alongside, and then put half the shiitake slices on to the chives.

7 Lift the makisu with your thumbs while pressing the fillings with your fingers and roll up gently.

8 When completed, gently roll the makisu on the chopping board to firm it up. Unwrap and set the *futo-maki* aside. Repeat the process to make another roll.

HOSO-MAKI (THIN-ROLLED SUSHI)
MAKES TWENTY-FOUR PIECES

INGREDIENTS
   2 nori sheets, cut in half crossways
   1 quantity *su-meshi*
   45ml/3 tbsp wasabi paste from a
      tube, or the same amount of wasabi
      powder mixed with 10ml/2 tsp
      water, plus extra for serving
For the fillings
   90g/3½oz very fresh tuna steak
   10cm/4in cucumber or 17cm/6½in
      Japanese cucumber
   5ml/1 tsp roasted sesame seeds
   6cm/2½in takuan, cut into 1cm/½in
      thick long strips

1 For the fillings, cut the tuna with the grain into 1cm/½in wide strips. Cut the cucumber into 1cm/½in thick strips.

2 Place the makisu on the work surface, then place a nori sheet on it horizontally, rough-side up. Spread a quarter of the *su-meshi* over the nori to cover evenly, leaving a 1cm/½in margin on the side furthest from you. Press firmly to smooth the surface.

3 Spread a little wasabi paste across the the rice and arrange some of the tuna strips horizontally in a row across the middle. Cut off the excess.

4 Hold the makisu with both hands and carefully roll it up, wrapping the tuna in the middle, and rolling away from the side closest to you. Hold the rolled makisu with both hands and squeeze gently to firm the *nori-maki*.

5 Slowly unwrap the makisu, remove the rolled tuna *hoso-maki* and set aside. Make another tuna *hoso-maki* with the remaining ingredients.

6 Repeat the same process using only the cucumber strips with the green skin on. Sprinkle sesame seeds on the cucumber before rolling.

7 Repeat with the takuan strips, but omit the wasabi paste. Keep the sushi on a slightly damp chopping board, covered with clear film (plastic wrap) during preparation. When finished, you should have two *hoso-maki* of tuna, and one each of cucumber and takuan.

To serve the *nori-maki*

1 Cut each *futo-maki* roll into eight pieces, using a very sharp knife. Wipe the knife with a dishtowel dampened with rice vinegar after each cut. Cut each *hoso-maki* into six pieces in the same way.

2 Line up all the *maki* on a large tray. Serve with small dishes of wasabi, gari, and shoyu for dipping.

COOK'S TIP
Half-fill a small bowl with water and add 30ml/2 tbsp rice vinegar. Use this to wet your hands to prevent the rice sticking when rolling sushi.

COMPRESSED SUSHI <u>WITH</u> SMOKED SALMON

THIS SUSHI, KNOWN AS OSHI-ZUSHI, DATES BACK ALMOST A THOUSAND YEARS. THE EARLIEST FORMS OF SUSHI WERE MADE AS A MEANS OF PRESERVING FISH. THE COOKED RICE WAS USED AS A MEDIUM TO PRODUCE LACTIC ACID AND WAS DISCARDED AFTER ONE YEAR. ONLY THE MARINATED FISH WAS EATEN.

2 Wet a wooden Japanese sushi mould or line a 25 × 7.5 × 5cm/10 × 3 × 2in plastic container with a large sheet of clear film (plastic wrap), allowing the edges to hang over.

3 Spread half the smoked salmon to evenly cover the bottom of the mould or container. Add a quarter of the cooked rice and firmly press down with your hands dampened with rice vinegar until it is 1cm/½in thick. Add the remainder of the salmon, and press the remaining rice on top.

4 Put the wet wooden lid on the mould, or cover the plastic container with the overhanging clear film. Place a weight, such as a heavy dinner plate, on top. Leave in a cool place overnight, or for at least 3 hours. If you keep it in the refrigerator, choose the least cool part.

5 Remove the compressed sushi from the mould or container and unwrap. Cut into 2cm/¾in slices and serve on a Japanese lacquered tray or a large plate. Quarter the lemon rings. Garnish with two slices of lemon on top of each piece and serve.

COOK'S TIPS
• You can also use smoked haddock instead of smoked salmon, if you like.
• If you don't have a mould or narrow container, use a container about 15cm/ 6in square. Cut the pressed sushi in half lengthways, then into 2cm/¾in slices. Cut the slices in half to make a nice canapé-type snack for a party.

MAKES ABOUT TWELVE

INGREDIENTS
 175g/6oz smoked salmon,
  thickly sliced
 15ml/1 tbsp sake
 15ml/1 tbsp water
 30ml/2 tbsp shoyu
 1 quantity *su-meshi*
 1 lemon, thinly sliced into 6 × 3mm/
  ⅛in rings

1 Lay the smoked salmon on a chopping board and sprinkle with a mixture of the sake, water and shoyu. Leave to marinate for an hour, then wipe dry with kitchen paper.

SU-MESHI <u>IN</u> TOFU BAGS

ABURA-AGE (FRIED THIN TOFU) IS DIFFERENT TO OTHER TOFU PRODUCTS. IT CAN BE OPENED UP LIKE A BAG, AND IN THIS RECIPE IT'S SERVED WITH SOY SAUCE-BASED SEASONINGS AND FILLED WITH SU-MESHI.

SERVES FOUR

INGREDIENTS

8 fresh abura-age or 275g/10oz can ready-to-use abura-age (contains 16 halves)
900ml/1½ pints/3¾ cups second dashi stock, or the same amount of water and 2 tsp dashi-no-moto
90ml/6 tbsp caster (superfine) sugar
30ml/2 tbsp sake
70ml/4½ tbsp shoyu
generous 1 quantity *su-meshi*, made with 40ml/8 tsp sugar
30ml/2 tbsp toasted white sesame seeds
gari, to garnish

1 Par-boil the fresh abura-age in rapidly boiling water for about 1 minute. Drain under running water and leave to cool. Squeeze the excess water out gently. Cut each sheet in half and carefully pull open the cut end to make bags. If you are using canned abura-age, drain the liquid.

2 Lay the abura-age bags in a large pan. Pour in the dashi stock to cover and bring to the boil. Reduce the heat and cover, then simmer for 20 minutes. Add the sugar in three batches during this time, shaking the pan to dissolve it. Simmer for a further 15 minutes.

3 Add the sake. Shake the pan again, and add the shoyu in three batches. Simmer until almost all the liquid has evaporated. Transfer the abura-age to a wide sieve and leave to drain.

4 Mix the *su-meshi* and sesame seeds in a wet mixing bowl. Wet your hands and take a little *su-meshi*. Shape it into a rectangular block. Open one abura-age bag and insert the block. Press the edges together to close the bag.

5 Once all the bags have been filled, place them on a large serving plate or individual plates with the bottom of the bag on top. Garnish with gari.

COOK'S TIP

To open the abura-age without breaking them, place them on a chopping board and, with the palm of your hand, rub them gently on the board. Then pull apart little by little from the cut end and work towards the bottom. When fully open, put your finger inside to make sure the corners are opened completely.

RICE BALLS WITH FOUR FILLINGS

ONIGIRI, THE JAPANESE NAME FOR THIS DISH, MEANS HAND-MOULDED RICE. JAPANESE RICE IS IDEAL FOR MAKING RICE BALLS, WHICH ARE FILLED HERE WITH SALMON, MACKEREL, UMEBOSHI AND OLIVES. THE NORI COATING MAKES THEM EASY TO PICK UP WITH YOUR FINGERS.

SERVES FOUR

INGREDIENTS
  50g/2oz salmon fillet, skinned
  3 umeboshi, 50g/2oz in total weight
  45ml/3 tbsp sesame seeds
  2.5ml/½ tsp mirin
  50g/2oz smoked mackerel fillet
  2 nori sheets, each cut into
    8 strips
  6 pitted black olives, wiped and
    finely chopped
  fine salt
  Japanese pickles, to serve
For the rice
  450g/1lb/2¼ cups Japanese short
    grain rice
  550ml/18fl oz/2½ cups water

1 To cook the rice, wash it thoroughly with cold water. Drain and put into a heavy pan. Pour in the water and leave for 30 minutes. Put the lid on tightly and bring the pan to the boil. Reduce the heat and simmer for 12 minutes. When you hear a crackling noise remove from the heat and leave to stand, covered, for about 15 minutes.

2 Stir carefully with a dampened rice paddle or wooden spatula to aerate the rice. Leave to cool for 30 minutes while you prepare the fillings. Thoroughly salt the salmon fillet and leave for at least 30 minutes.

3 Stone (pit) the umeboshi. With the back of a fork, mash them slightly. Mix with 15ml/1 tbsp of the sesame seeds and the mirin to make a rough paste.

4 Wash the salt from the salmon. Grill (broil) the salmon and smoked mackerel under a high heat. Using a fork, remove the skin and divide the fish into loose, chunky flakes. Keep the salmon and mackerel pieces separate.

5 Toast the remaining sesame seeds in a dry frying pan over a low heat until they start to pop.

6 Check the temperature of the rice. It should be still quite warm but not hot. To start moulding, you need a teacup and a bowl of cold water to wet your hands. Put the teacup and tablespoons for measuring into the water. Put fine salt into a small dish. Wipe a chopping board with a very wet dishtowel. Wash your hands thoroughly with unperfumed soap and dry.

7 Remove the teacup from the bowl and shake off excess water. Scoop about 30ml/2 tbsp rice into the teacup. With your fingers, make a well in the centre of the rice and put in a quarter of the salmon flakes. Cover the salmon with another 15ml/1 tbsp rice. Press well.

8 Wet your hands and sprinkle them with a pinch of salt. Rub it all over your palms. Turn the rice in the teacup out into one hand and squeeze the rice shape with both hands to make a densely packed flat ball.

9 Wrap the rice ball with a nori strip. Put on to the chopping board. Make three more balls using the remaining salmon, then make four balls using the smoked mackerel and another four balls using the umeboshi paste.

10 Scoop about 45ml/3 tbsp rice into the teacup. Mix in a quarter of the chopped olives. Press the rice with your fingers. Wet your hands with water and rub with a pinch of salt and a quarter of the toasted sesame seeds. Turn the teacup on to one hand and shape the rice mixture into a ball as above. The sesame seeds should stick to the rice. This time, do not wrap with nori. Repeat, making three more balls.

11 Serve one of each kind of rice ball on individual plates with a small helping of Japanese pickles.

RED RICE WRAPPED IN OAK LEAVES

THIS STICKY RICE DISH, SEKIHAN, IS COOKED FOR SPECIAL OCCASIONS AND TAKES 8 HOURS TO PREPARE. EDIBLE KASHIWA (OAK) LEAVES ARE USED WHEN PREPARED FOR A BOY-CHILD'S FESTIVAL.

SERVES FOUR

INGREDIENTS

65g/2½oz/⅓ cup dried azuki beans
5ml/1 tsp salt
300g/11oz/1½ cups mochigome
50g/2oz/¼ cup Japanese short
   grain rice
12 salted kashiwa leaves (optional)
For the *goma-shio*
45ml/3 tbsp sesame seeds (black
   sesame, if available)
5ml/1 tsp ground sea salt

1 Put the azuki beans in a heavy pan and pour in 400ml/14fl oz/1⅔ cups plus 20ml/4 tsp water.

2 Bring to the boil, reduce the heat and simmer, covered, for 20–30 minutes, or until the beans look swollen but are still firm. Remove from the heat and drain. Reserve the liquid in a bowl and add the salt. Return the beans to the pan.

3 Wash the two rices together. Drain in a sieve and leave for 30 minutes.

4 Bring another 400ml/14fl oz/1⅔ cups plus 20ml/4 tsp water to the boil. Add to the beans and boil, then simmer for 30 minutes. The beans' skins should start to crack. Drain and add the liquid to the bowl with the reserved liquid. Cover the beans and leave to cool.

5 Add the rice to the bean liquid. Leave to soak for 4–5 hours. Drain the rice and reserve the liquid. Mix the beans into the rice.

6 Bring a steamer of water to the boil. Turn off the heat. Place a tall glass upside down in the centre of the steaming compartment. Pour the rice and beans into the steamer and gently pull the glass out. The hole in the middle will allow even distribution of the steam. Steam on high for 10 minutes.

7 Using your fingers, sprinkle the rice mixture with the reserved liquid from the bowl. Cover again and repeat the process twice more at 10 minute intervals, then leave to steam for 15 minutes more. Remove from the heat. Leave to stand for 10 minutes.

8 Make the *goma-shio*. Roast the sesame seeds and salt in a dry frying pan until the seeds start to pop. Leave to cool, then put in a small dish.

9 Wipe each kashiwa leaf with a wet dishtowel. Scoop 120ml/4fl oz/½ cup of the rice mixture into a wet tea cup and press with wet fingers. Turn the cup upside down and shape the moulded rice with your hands into a flat ball. Insert into a leaf folded in two. Repeat this process until all the leaves are used. Alternatively, transfer the red rice to a large bowl wiped with a wet towel.

10 Serve the red rice with a sprinkle of *goma-shio*. The kashiwa leaves (salted, not fresh) are edible.

FIVE INGREDIENTS RICE

THE JAPANESE LOVE RICE SO MUCH THEY INVENTED MANY WAYS TO ENJOY IT. HERE, CHICKEN AND VEGETABLES ARE COOKED WITH SHORT GRAIN RICE MAKING A HEALTHY LIGHT LUNCH DISH CALLED KAYAKU-GOHAN. SERVE WITH A SIMPLE, CLEAR SOUP AND TANGY PICKLES.

SERVES FOUR

INGREDIENTS
    275g/10oz/1⅓ cups Japanese short
      grain rice
    90g/3½oz carrot, peeled
    2.5ml/½ tsp lemon juice
    90g/3½oz gobo or canned
      bamboo shoots
    225g/8oz oyster mushrooms
    8 mitsuba sprigs, root part removed
    350ml/12fl oz/1½ cups second dashi
      stock, or the same amount of water
      and 7.5ml/1½ tsp dashi-no-moto
    150g/5oz chicken breast portion,
      skinned, boned and cut into 2cm/
      ¾in dice
    30ml/2 tbsp shoyu
    30ml/2 tbsp sake
    25ml/1½ tbsp mirin
    pinch of salt

1 Put the rice in a large bowl and wash well with cold water. Change the water until it becomes clear. Tip the rice into a sieve and leave to drain for 30 minutes.

2 Using a sharp knife, cut the carrot into 5mm/¼in rounds, then cut the discs into flowers.

COOK'S TIP
Although gobo or burdock is recognized as a poisonous plant in the West, the Japanese have long been eating it, but it must be cooked. It contains iron and other acidic elements that are harmful if eaten raw, but after soaking in alkaline water and cooking for a short time, gobo is no longer poisonous.

3 Fill a small bowl with cold water and add the lemon juice. Peel the gobo and then slice with a knife as if you were sharpening a pencil into the bowl. Leave for 15 minutes, then drain. If using canned bamboo shoots, slice into thin matchsticks.

4 Tear the oyster mushrooms into thin strips. Chop the mitsuba sprigs into 2cm/¾in long pieces. Put them in a sieve and pour over hot water from the kettle to wilt them. Allow to drain and then set aside.

5 Heat the dashi stock in a large pan and add the carrots and gobo or bamboo shoots. Bring to the boil and add the chicken. Remove any scum from the surface, and add the shoyu, sake, mirin and salt.

6 Add the rice and mushrooms and cover with a tight-fitting lid. Bring back to the boil, wait 5 minutes, then reduce the heat and simmer for 10 minutes. Remove from the heat without lifting the lid and leave to stand for 15 minutes. Add the mitsuba and serve.

BROWN RICE AND MUSHROOMS IN CLEAR SOUP

THIS IS A GOOD AND QUICK WAY OF USING UP LEFTOVER RICE. IN THIS HEARTY DISH, KNOWN AS GENMAI ZOUSUI, BROWN RICE IS USED FOR ITS NUTTY FLAVOUR. SHORT GRAIN JAPANESE OR ITALIAN BROWN RICE, WHICH CAN BE FOUND IN HEALTH-FOOD STORES, ARE BEST FOR THIS RECIPE.

SERVES FOUR

INGREDIENTS
1 litre/1¾ pints/4 cups second dashi
 stock, or the same amount of water
 and 20ml/4 tsp dashi-no-moto
60ml/4 tbsp sake
5ml/1 tsp salt
60ml/4 tbsp shoyu
115g/4oz fresh shiitake mushrooms,
 thinly sliced
300g/11oz cooked brown rice (see
 Cook's Tip)
2 large (US extra large) eggs, beaten
30ml/2 tbsp chopped fresh chives
For the garnish
15ml/1 tbsp sesame seeds
shichimi togarashi (optional)

1 Mix the dashi stock, sake, salt and shoyu in a large pan. Bring to the boil, then add the sliced shiitake. Cook for 5 minutes over a medium heat.

2 Add the cooked brown rice to the pan and stir gently over a medium heat with a wooden spoon. Break up any large chunks, and thoroughly warm the rice through.

3 Pour the beaten eggs into the pan as if drawing a whirlpool. Lower the heat and cover. Do not stir.

4 Remove the pan from the heat after about 3 minutes, and allow to stand for 3 minutes more. The egg should be just cooked. Sprinkle the chopped chives into the pan.

5 Serve the dish in individual bowls. Garnish with sesame seeds and shichimi togarashi, if you like.

COOK'S TIP
To cook brown rice, wash and drain, then put 2 parts water to 1 part rice into a pan. Bring to the boil, cover, then simmer for 40 minutes, or until the water has been absorbed. Leave to stand, covered, for 5 minutes.

RICE IN GREEN TEA WITH SALMON

A FAST FOOD, OCHA-ZUKE IS A COMMON JAPANESE SNACK TO HAVE AFTER DRINKS AND NIBBLES. IN THE KYOTO REGION, OFFERING THIS DISH TO GUESTS USED TO BE A POLITE WAY OF SAYING THE PARTY WAS OVER. THE GUESTS WERE EXPECTED TO DECLINE THE OFFER AND LEAVE IMMEDIATELY!

SERVES FOUR

INGREDIENTS
150g/5oz salmon fillet
¼ nori sheet
250g/9oz/1¼ cups Japanese short
 grain rice cooked using 350ml/
 12fl oz/1½ cups water
15ml/1 tbsp sencha leaves
5ml/1 tsp wasabi paste from a tube,
 or 5ml/1 tsp wasabi powder mixed
 with 1.5ml/¼ tsp water (optional)
20ml/4 tsp shoyu
salt

1 Thoroughly salt the salmon fillet and leave for 30 minutes. If the salmon fillet is thicker than 2.5cm/1in, slice it in half and salt both halves.

2 Wipe the salt off the salmon with kitchen paper and grill (broil) the fish under a preheated grill (broiler) for about 5 minutes until cooked through. Remove the skin and any bones, then roughly flake the salmon with a fork.

3 Using scissors, cut the nori into short, narrow strips about 20 x 5mm/¾ x ¼in long, or leave as long narrow strips, if you prefer.

4 If the cooked rice is warm, put equal amounts into individual rice bowls or soup bowls. If the rice is cold, put in a sieve and pour hot water from a kettle over it to warm it up. Drain and pour into the bowls. Place the salmon pieces on top of the rice.

5 Put the sencha leaves in a teapot. Bring 600ml/1 pint/2½ cups water to the boil, remove from the heat and allow to cool slightly. Pour into the teapot and wait for 45 seconds. Strain the tea gently and evenly over the top of the rice and salmon. Add some nori and wasabi, if using, to the top of the rice, then trickle shoyu over and serve.

LUNCH-BOX RICE <u>WITH</u> THREE TOPPINGS

SAN-SHOKU BENTO IS A TYPICAL BENTO (LUNCH-BOX) MENU FOR JAPANESE CHILDREN. COLOURFUL TOPPINGS AND A VARIETY OF TASTES HOLD THEIR ATTENTION SO THEY DON'T GET BORED.

MAKES FOUR LUNCH BOXES

INGREDIENTS
   275g/10oz/scant 1½ cups Japanese
      short grain rice cooked using 375ml/
      13fl oz/scant 1⅔ cups water, cooled
   45ml/3 tbsp sesame seeds, toasted
   salt
   3 mangetouts (snow peas), to garnish
For the *iri-tamago* (yellow topping)
   30ml/2 tbsp caster (superfine) sugar
   5ml/1 tsp salt
   3 large (US extra large) eggs, beaten
For the *denbu* (pink topping)
   115g/4oz cod fillet, skinned
      and boned
   20ml/4 tsp caster (superfine) sugar
   5ml/1 tsp salt
   5ml/1 tsp sake
   2 drops of red vegetable colouring,
      diluted with a few drops of water
For the *tori-soboro* (beige topping)
   200g/7oz minced (ground)
      raw chicken
   45ml/3 tbsp sake
   15ml/1 tbsp caster (superfine) sugar
   15ml/1 tbsp shoyu
   15ml/1 tbsp water

1 To make the *iri-tamago*, add the sugar and salt to the eggs in a pan. Cook over a medium heat, stirring with a whisk or fork as you would to scramble an egg. When it is almost set, remove from the heat and stir until the egg becomes fine and slightly dry.

2 To make the *denbu*, cook the cod fillet for 2 minutes in a large pan of boiling water. Drain and dry well with kitchen paper. Skin and remove all the fish bones.

3 Put the cod and sugar into a pan, add the salt and sake, and cook over a low heat for 1 minute, stirring with a fork to flake the cod. Reduce the heat to low and sprinkle on the colouring. Continue to stir for 15–20 minutes, or until the cod flakes become very fluffy and fibrous. Transfer the *denbu* to a plate.

4 To make the *tori-soboro*, put the minced chicken, sake, sugar, shoyu and water into a small pan. Cook over a medium heat for about 3 minutes, then reduce the heat to medium-low and stir with a fork or whisk until the liquid has almost evaporated.

5 Blanch the mangetouts for about 3 minutes in lightly salted boiling water, drain and carefully slice into fine 3mm/⅛in sticks.

6 Mix the rice with the sesame seeds in a bowl. With a wet spoon, divide the rice among four 17 × 12cm/6½ × 4½in lunch boxes. Flatten the surface using the back of a wooden spoon.

7 Spoon a quarter of the egg into each box to cover a third of the rice. Cover the next third with a quarter of the *denbu*, and the last section with a quarter of the chicken topping. Use the lid to divide the boxes, if you like. Garnish with the mangetout sticks.

CHICKEN AND EGG ON RICE

THIS DISH IS CALLED OYAKO DON, *WHICH MEANS A PARENT (THE CHICKEN) AND A CHILD (THE EGG). IT IS TRADITIONALLY COOKED IN A DON-BURI, WHICH IS A DEEP, ROUND CERAMIC BOWL WITH A LID, AND IS ESSENTIAL TABLEWARE IN JAPAN; RESTAURANTS OFTEN USE THEM IN LUNCHTIME MENUS.*

SERVES FOUR

INGREDIENTS

250g/9oz chicken thighs, skinned
  and boned
4 mitsuba sprigs or a handful of
  mustard and cress
300ml/½ pint/1¼ cups second dashi
  stock, or the same amount of water
  and 25ml/1½ tbsp dashi-no-moto
30ml/2 tbsp caster (superfine) sugar
60ml/4 tbsp mirin
60ml/4 tbsp shoyu
2 small onions, sliced
  thinly lengthways
4 large (US extra large) eggs, beaten
275g/10oz/scant 1½ cups Japanese
  short grain rice cooked with 375ml/
  13fl oz/scant 1⅔ cups water
shichimi togarashi, to serve (optional)

1 Cut the chicken thighs into 2cm/¾in square bitesize chunks. Remove the root part from the mitsuba, and chop into 2.5cm/1in lengths.

2 Pour the dashi stock, sugar, mirin and shoyu into a clean frying pan with a lid and bring to the boil. Add the onion slices and lay the chicken pieces on top. Cook over a high heat for 5 minutes, shaking the pan frequently.

3 When the chicken is cooked, sprinkle with the mitsuba or mustard and cress, and pour the beaten eggs over to cover the chicken. Cover and wait for 30 seconds. Do not stir.

4 Remove from the heat and leave to stand for 1 minute. The egg should be just cooked but still soft, rather than set. Do not leave it so that the egg becomes a firm omelette.

5 Scoop the warm rice on to individual plates, then pour the soft eggs and chicken on to the rice. Serve immediately with a little shichimi-togarashi, if a spicy taste is desired.

COOK'S TIP
Ideally, this dish should be cooked in individual shallow pans with lids. A small omelette pan can work perfectly well.

SOUPS AND NOODLES

Soups, a showcase of the season in miniature, are usually

eaten with or at the end of the meal. Apart from ramen,

Japanese noodles are quite different to the Chinese, and the

soup stock is made with great care to set off their flavour.

Buckwheat noodles in particular have a very delicate aroma,

and are eaten with a simple dipping sauce.

MISO SOUP

ESSENTIAL TO ANY JAPANESE MEAL IS A BOWL OF RICE. NEXT IS MISO SOUP, SERVED IN A LACQUERED BOWL. OF THE MANY VARIATIONS, WAKAME TO TOFU NO MISO-SHIRU *DEFINITELY COMES FIRST.*

SERVES FOUR

INGREDIENTS
   5g/⅛oz dried wakame
   ½ × 225–285g/8–10¼oz packet fresh
     soft tofu or long-life silken tofu
   400ml/14fl oz/1⅔ cups second dashi
     stock or the same amount of water
     and 5ml/1 tsp dashi-no-moto
   45ml/3 tbsp miso
   2 spring onions (scallions),
     finely chopped
   shichimi togarashi or sansho
     (optional), to serve

1 Soak the wakame in a large bowl of cold water for 15 minutes. Drain and chop into stamp-size pieces if using the long or broad type.

2 Cut the tofu into 1cm/½in strips, then cut horizontally through the strips. Cut the thin strips into squares.

3 Bring the dashi stock to the boil. Put the miso in a small cup and mix with 60ml/4 tbsp hot stock from the pan. Reduce the heat to low and pour two-thirds of the miso into the pan of stock.

4 Taste the soup and add more miso if required. Add the wakame and the tofu and increase the heat. Just before the soup comes to the boil again, add the spring onions and remove from the heat. Do not boil. Serve sprinkled with shichimi togarashi or sansho, if liked.

COOK'S TIPS
• To make first dashi stock, put a 10cm/4in square piece of dried konbu into a pan. Pour in 600ml/1 pint/2½ cups water and soak for an hour. Heat to near boiling point, then remove from the heat. Remove and reserve the konbu for the second dashi. Add 20g/¾oz kezuri-bushi to the pan and heat on low. Do not stir. Just before it reaches boiling point, turn off the heat. Allow the flakes to settle down to the bottom of the pan. Strain and reserve the kezuri-bushi flakes for the second dashi stock.
• To make second dashi stock, put the reserved konbu and kezuri-bushi from the first dashi into a pan with 600ml/1 pint/2½ cups water. Bring to the boil, then simmer for 15 minutes until the stock is reduced by a third. Add 15g/½oz kezuri-bushi to the pan. Immediately remove from the heat. Skim any scum from the surface. Leave to stand for 10 minutes, then strain.

CLEAR SOUP WITH SEAFOOD STICKS

THIS DELICATE SOUP, CALLED O-SUMASHI, *WHICH IS OFTEN EATEN WITH SUSHI, IS VERY QUICK TO MAKE IF YOU PREPARE THE FIRST DASHI BEFOREHAND OR IF YOU USE FREEZE-DRIED DASHI-NO-MOTO.*

SERVES FOUR

INGREDIENTS
4 mitsuba sprigs or 4 chives and a
  few sprigs of mustard and cress
4 seafood sticks
400ml/14fl oz/1⅔ cups first dashi
  stock, or the same amount of water
  and 5ml/1 tsp dashi-no-moto
15ml/1 tbsp shoyu
7.5ml/1½ tsp salt
grated rind of yuzu (optional),
  to garnish

1 Mitsuba leaves are normally sold with the stems and roots on to retain freshness. Cut off the root, then cut 5cm/2in from the top, retaining both the long straw-like stem and the leaf.

2 Blanch the stems in hot water from the kettle. If you use chives, choose them at least 10cm/4in in length and blanch them, too.

3 Take a seafood stick and carefully tie around the middle with a mitsuba stem or chive, holding it in place with a knot. Do not pull too tightly, as the bow will easily break. Repeat the process to make four tied seafood sticks.

4 Hold one seafood stick in your hand. With your finger, carefully loosen both ends to make it look like a tassel.

5 Place one seafood stick in each soup bowl, then put the four mitsuba leaves or mustard and cress on top.

6 Heat the stock in a pan and bring to the boil. Add shoyu and salt to taste. Pour the stock gently over the mitsuba and seafood stick. Sprinkle with grated yuzu rind, if using.

VARIATION
You can use small prawns (shrimp) instead of seafood sticks. Blanch 12 raw prawns in boiling water until they curl up and form a full circle. Drain. Tie mitsuba stems to make four bows. Arrange three prawns side by side in each bowl and put the mitsuba bows and leaves on top.

MISO SOUP WITH PORK AND VEGETABLES

THIS IS QUITE A RICH AND FILLING SOUP. ITS JAPANESE NAME, TANUKI JIRU, MEANS RACCOON SOUP FOR HUNTERS, BUT AS RACCOONS ARE NOT EATEN NOWADAYS, PORK IS NOW USED.

SERVES FOUR

INGREDIENTS
200g/7oz lean boneless pork
15cm/6in piece gobo or 1 parsnip
50g/2oz daikon
4 fresh shiitake mushrooms
½ konnyaku or ½ × 225–285g/
    8–10¼oz packet tofu
a little sesame oil, for stir-frying
600ml/1 pint/2½ cups second dashi
    stock, or the same amount of water
    and 10ml/2 tsp dashi-no-moto
70ml/4½ tbsp miso
2 spring onions (scallions), chopped
5ml/1 tsp sesame seeds

1 Press the meat down on a chopping board using the palm of your hand and slice horizontally into very thin long strips, then cut the strips crossways into stamp-size pieces. Set the pork aside.

2 Peel the gobo using a potato peeler, then cut diagonally into 1cm/½in thick slices. Quickly plunge the slices into a bowl of cold water to stop them discolouring. If you are using parsnip, peel, cut it in half lengthways, then cut it into 1cm/½in thick half-moon-shaped slices.

3 Peel and slice the daikon into 1.5cm/⅔in thick discs. Cut the discs into 1.5cm/⅔in cubes. Remove the shiitake stalks and cut the caps into quarters.

4 Place the konnyaku in a pan of boiling water and cook for 1 minute. Drain and cool. Cut in quarters lengthways, then crossways into 3mm/⅛in thick pieces.

5 Heat a little sesame oil in a heavy cast-iron or enamelled pan until purple smoke rises. Stir-fry the pork, then add the tofu, if using, the konnyaku and all the vegetables except for the spring onions. When the colour of the meat has changed, add the stock.

6 Bring to the boil over a medium heat, and skim off the foam until the soup looks fairly clear. Reduce the heat, cover, and simmer for 15 minutes.

7 Put the miso in a small bowl, and mix with 60ml/4 tbsp hot stock to make a smooth paste. Stir one-third of the miso into the soup. Taste and add more miso if required. Add the spring onion and remove from the heat. Serve very hot in individual soup bowls and sprinkle with sesame seeds.

NEW YEAR'S SOUP

THE ELABORATE NEW YEAR'S DAY CELEBRATION BRUNCH STARTS WITH A TINY GLASS OF SPICED WARM SAKE, O-TOSO. THEN, THIS NEW YEAR'S SOUP, O-ZONI, AND OTHER FESTIVE DISHES ARE SERVED.

SERVES FOUR

INGREDIENTS
4 dried shiitake mushrooms
300g/11oz chicken thighs, bones removed and reserved
300g/11oz salmon fillet, skin on, scaled
30ml/2 tbsp sake
50g/2oz satoimo or Jerusalem artichokes
50g/2oz daikon, peeled
50g/2oz carrots, peeled
4 spring onions (scallions), white part only, trimmed
4 mitsuba sprigs, root part removed
1 yuzu or lime
4 large raw tiger prawns (shrimp), peeled, but with tails left on
30ml/2 tbsp shoyu
8 canned gingko nuts (optional)
8 mochi slices
salt

1 First, make the soup stock. Soak the dried shiitake overnight in 1 litre/1¾ pints/4 cups cold water. Remove the softened shiitake and pour the water into a pan. Bring to the boil, add the chicken bones, then reduce the heat to medium. Skim frequently to remove scum. After 20 minutes, reduce the heat to low. Simmer for 30 minutes or until the liquid has reduced by a third. Strain the stock into another pan.

2 Chop the chicken and salmon into small bitesize cubes. Par-boil them both in boiling water with 15ml/1 tbsp sake for 1 minute. Drain and wash off the scum under cold water.

3 Scrub the satoimo or artichokes with a hard brush, and thickly peel. Put in a pan and add enough water to cover. Add a pinch of salt and bring to the boil. Reduce the heat to medium, cook for 15 minutes and drain. Rinse the satoimo (to remove the sticky juice) or artichokes under running water. Wipe gently with kitchen paper. Cut the satoimo or artichokes, daikon and carrots into 1cm/½in cubes.

4 Remove and discard the stalks from the soaked shiitake, and slice the caps thinly. Chop the white part of the spring onions into 2.5cm/1in lengths.

5 Put the mitsuba sprigs into a sieve and pour hot water over them. Divide the leaf and stalk parts. Take a stalk and fold it into two, then tie it in the middle to make a bow. Make four bows.

6 Cut the yuzu or lime into four 3mm/⅛in thick round slices. Hollow out the inside to make rings of peel.

7 Add the remaining sake to the soup stock and bring to the boil. Add the daikon, carrot and shiitake, then reduce the heat to medium and cook for 15 minutes.

8 Put the prawns, satoimo or artichokes, spring onions, chicken and salmon into the pan. Wait for 5 minutes, then add the shoyu. Reduce the heat to low and add the gingko nuts, if using.

9 Cut the mochi in half crossways. Toast under a moderate preheated grill (broiler). Turn every minute until both sides are golden and the pieces have started to swell like a balloon; this will take about 5 minutes.

10 Quickly place the toasted mochi in individual soup bowls and pour the hot soup over the top. Arrange a mitsuba leaf in the centre of each bowl, put a yuzu or lime ring on top, and lay a mitsuba bow across. Serve immediately.

SOBA NOODLES IN HOT SOUP WITH TEMPURA

WHEN YOU COOK JAPANESE NOODLE DISHES, EVERYONE SHOULD BE READY AT THE DINNER TABLE, BECAUSE COOKED NOODLES START TO SOFTEN AND LOSE THEIR TASTE AND TEXTURE QUITE QUICKLY.

SERVES FOUR

INGREDIENTS
    400g/14oz dried soba noodles
    1 spring onion (scallion), sliced
    shichimi togarashi (optional)
For the tempura
    16 medium raw tiger or king prawns
        (jumbo shrimp), heads and shell
        removed, tails intact
    400ml/14fl oz/1⅔ cups ice-cold water
    1 large (US extra large) egg, beaten
    200g/7oz/scant 2 cups plain
        (all-purpose) flour
    vegetable oil, for deep-frying
For the soup
    150ml/¼ pint/⅔ cup mirin
    150ml/¼ pint/⅔ cup shoyu
    900ml/1½ pints/3¾ cups water
    25g/1oz kezuri-bushi or 2 × 15g/
        ½oz packets
    15ml/1 tbsp caster (superfine) sugar
    5ml/1 tsp salt
    900ml/1½ pints/3¾ cups first dashi
        stock or the same amount of water
        and 12.5ml/2½ tsp dashi-no-moto

1 To make the soup, put the mirin in a large pan. Bring to the boil, then add the rest of the soup ingredients apart from the dashi stock. Bring back to the boil, then reduce the heat to low. Skim off the scum and cook for 2 minutes. Strain the soup and put back into a clean pan with the dashi stock.

2 Remove the vein from the prawns, then make 5 shallow cuts into each prawn's belly. Clip the tip of the tail with scissors and squeeze out any moisture from the tail.

3 To make the batter, pour the ice-cold water into a bowl and mix in the beaten egg. Sift in the flour and stir briefly; it should remain fairly lumpy.

4 Heat the oil in a wok or deep-fryer to 180°C/350°F. Hold the tail of a prawn, dunk it in the batter, then plunge it into the hot oil. Deep-fry 2 prawns at a time until crisp and golden. Drain on kitchen paper and keep warm.

5 Put the noodles in a large pan with at least 2 litres/3½ pints/9 cups rapidly boiling water, and stir frequently to stop them sticking.

6 When the water foams, pour in about 50ml/2fl oz/¼ cup cold water to lower the temperature. Repeat when the water foams once again. The noodles should be slightly softer than *al dente* pasta. Tip the noodles into a sieve and wash under cold water with your hands to rinse off any oil.

7 Heat the soup. Warm the noodles with hot water, and divide among individual serving bowls. Place the prawns attractively on the noodles and add the soup. Sprinkle with sliced spring onion and some shichimi togarashi, if you like. Serve immediately.

BUCKWHEAT NOODLES WITH DIPPING SAUCE

COLD SOBA NOODLES ARE OFTEN EATEN IN SUMMER AND SERVED ON A BAMBOO TRAY WITH A DIPPING SAUCE. THE JAPANESE LOVE THE TASTE OF THE NOODLES; THE SAUCE ENHANCES THEIR FLAVOUR.

SERVES FOUR

INGREDIENTS

4 spring onions (scallions),
  finely chopped
½ nori sheet, about 10cm/4in square
400g/14oz dried soba noodles
5ml/1 tsp wasabi paste from a tube,
  or 5ml/1 tsp wasabi powder mixed
  with 2.5ml/½ tsp water
For the dipping sauce
30g/1¼oz kezuri-bushi
200ml/7fl oz/scant 1 cup shoyu
200ml/7fl oz/scant 1 cup mirin
750ml/1¼ pints/3 cups water

1 To make the dipping sauce, mix all the ingredients in a small pan. Bring to the boil, and cook for 2 minutes. Reduce the heat to medium, and cook for a further 2 minutes. Strain through muslin (cheesecloth). Cool, then chill.

2 Soak the spring onions in ice-cold water in a bowl for 5 minutes. Drain and squeeze out the excess water.

3 Toast the nori over a medium flame until dry and crisp, then cut it into short strips, 3mm/⅛in wide, with scissors.

4 Heat 2 litres/3½ pints/9 cups water in a large pan. The water should not fill more than two-thirds of the pan's depth.

5 Bring to the boil, then add the soba. Distribute the noodles evenly in the pan, and stir to prevent them sticking. When the water is bubbling, pour in about 50ml/2fl oz/¼ cup cold water to lower the temperature.

6 Repeat this process and cook for the length of time stated on the packet, or about 5 minutes. To test if the noodles are ready, pick one out and cut it with your finger. It should be just tender to the touch.

7 Put a large sieve under cold running water. Pour the cooked soba into the sieve, and wash thoroughly with your hands. Rub the soba well to remove the starch; the soba should feel slightly elastic. Drain again.

8 Pour the cold dipping sauce into four cups. Put the wasabi and spring onions into individual dishes for each guest. Divide the soba among four plates or baskets. Sprinkle with nori strips and serve cold, with the sauce, wasabi and spring onions.

9 Instruct each guest to mix the wasabi and onions into the dipping sauce. To eat, hold the dipping-sauce cup in one hand. Pick up a mouthful of soba from the basket or plate using chopsticks and dip the end into the dipping sauce, then slurp the noodles in with your lips.

COOK'S TIP
Other condiment ideas include yuzu or lime rind, finely grated radish, thinly sliced garlic or grated fresh root ginger.

UDON NOODLES WITH EGG BROTH AND GINGER

IN THIS DISH, CALLED ANKAKE UDON, THE SOUP FOR THE UDON IS THICKENED WITH CORNFLOUR AND RETAINS ITS HEAT FOR A LONG TIME. A PERFECT LUNCH FOR A FREEZING COLD DAY.

2 Heat at least 2 litres/3½ pints/9 cups water in a large pan, and cook the udon for 8 minutes or according to the packet instructions. Drain under cold running water and wash off the starch with your hands. Leave the udon in the sieve.

3 Pour the soup into a large pan and bring to the boil. Blend the cornflour with 60ml/4 tbsp water. Reduce the heat to medium and gradually add the cornflour mixture to the hot soup. Stir constantly. The soup will thicken after a few minutes. Reduce the heat to low.

4 Mix the egg, mustard and cress, and spring onions in a small bowl. Stir the soup once again to create a whirlpool. Pour the eggs slowly into the soup pan.

5 Reheat the udon with hot water from a kettle. Divide among four bowls and pour the soup over the top. Garnish with the ginger and serve hot.

SERVES FOUR

INGREDIENTS
    400g/14oz dried udon noodles
    30ml/2 tbsp cornflour (cornstarch)
    4 eggs, beaten
    50g/2oz mustard and cress
    2 spring onions (scallions),
        finely chopped
    2.5cm/1in fresh root ginger, peeled
        and finely grated, to garnish
For the soup
    1 litre/1¾ pints/4 cups water
    40g/1½oz kezuri-bushi
    25ml/1½ tbsp mirin
    25ml/1½ tbsp shoyu
    7.5ml/1½ tsp salt

1 To make the soup, place the water and the soup ingredients in a pan and bring to the boil on a medium heat. Remove from the heat when it starts boiling. Stand for 1 minute, then strain through muslin (cheesecloth). Check the taste and add more salt if required.

COOK'S TIP
You can use ready-made noodle soup, available from Japanese food stores. Follow the instructions to dilute with water or use straight from the bottle.

POT-COOKED UDON <u>IN</u> MISO SOUP

UDON IS A WHITE WHEAT NOODLE, MORE POPULAR IN THE SOUTH AND WEST OF JAPAN THAN THE NORTH. IT IS EATEN WITH VARIOUS HOT AND COLD SAUCES AND SOUPS. HERE, IN THIS DISH KNOWN AS MISO NIKOMI UDON, THE NOODLES ARE COOKED IN A CLAY POT WITH A RICH MISO SOUP.

SERVES FOUR

INGREDIENTS
200g/7oz chicken breast portion,
  boned and skinned
10ml/2 tsp sake
2 abura-age
900ml/1½ pints/3¾ cups second
  dashi stock, or the same amount
  of water and 7.5ml/1½ tsp
  dashi-no-moto
6 large fresh shiitake mushrooms,
  stalks removed, quartered
4 spring onions (scallions), trimmed
  and chopped into 3mm/⅛in lengths
30ml/2 tbsp mirin
about 90g/3½oz aka miso or
  hatcho miso
300g/11oz dried udon noodles
4 eggs
shichimi togarashi (optional)

1 Cut the chicken into bitesize pieces. Sprinkle with sake and leave to marinate for 15 minutes.

2 Put the abura-age in a sieve and thoroughly rinse with hot water from the kettle to wash off the oil. Drain on kitchen paper and cut each abura-age into 4 squares.

3 To make the soup, heat the second dashi stock in a large pan. When it has come to the boil, add the chicken pieces, shiitake mushrooms and abura-age and cook for 5 minutes. Remove the pan from the heat and add the spring onions.

4 Put the mirin and miso paste into a small bowl. Scoop 30ml/2 tbsp soup from the pan and mix this in well.

5 To cook the udon, boil at least 2 litres/3½ pints/9 cups water in a large pan. The water should not come higher than two-thirds the depth of the pan. Cook the udon for 6 minutes and drain.

6 Put the udon in one large flameproof clay pot or casserole (or divide among four small pots). Mix the miso paste into the soup and check the taste. Add more miso if required. Ladle in enough soup to cover the udon, and arrange the soup ingredients on top of the udon.

7 Put the soup on a medium heat and break an egg on top. When the soup bubbles, wait for 1 minute, then cover and remove from the heat. Leave to stand for 2 minutes. Serve with shichimi togarashi, if you like.

COLD SOMEN NOODLES

AT THE HEIGHT OF SUMMER, HIYA SOMEN — COLD SOMEN NOODLES SERVED IMMERSED IN COLD WATER WITH ICE CUBES AND ACCOMPANIED BY SAUCES AND RELISHES — ARE A REFRESHING MEAL.

SERVES FOUR

INGREDIENTS
  300g/11oz dried somen noodles
For the dipping sauce
  105ml/7 tbsp mirin
  2.5ml/½ tsp salt
  105ml/7 tbsp shoyu
  20g/¾oz kezuri-bushi
  400ml/14fl oz/1⅔ cups water
For the relishes
  2 spring onions (scallions), trimmed
    and finely chopped
  2.5cm/1in fresh root ginger, peeled
    and finely grated
  2 shiso leaves, finely chopped
    (optional)
  30ml/2 tbsp toasted sesame seeds
For the garnishes
  10cm/4in cucumber (a small salad
    cucumber is the best)
  5ml/1 tsp salt
  ice cubes or a block of ice
  ice-cold water
  115g/4oz cooked, peeled small
    prawns (shrimp)
  orchid flowers or nasturtium flowers
    and leaves

1 To make the dipping sauce, put the mirin in a medium pan and bring to the boil to evaporate the alcohol. Add the salt and shoyu and shake the pan gently to mix. Add the kezuri-bushi and mix with the liquid. Add the water and bring to the boil. Cook over vigorous heat for 3 minutes without stirring. Remove from the heat and strain through muslin or a jelly bag. Leave to cool, then chill in the refrigerator for at least an hour before serving.

2 Prepare the cucumber garnish. If the cucumber is bigger than 4cm/1½in in diameter, cut in half and scoop out the seeds, then slice thinly. For a smaller cucumber, first cut into 5cm/2in lengths, then use a vegetable peeler to remove the seeds and make a hole in the centre. Slice thinly. Sprinkle with the salt and leave in a sieve for 20 minutes, then rinse in cold water and drain.

3 Bring at least 1.5 litres/2½ pints/ 6¼ cups water to the boil in a large pan. Meanwhile, untie the bundle of somen. Have 75ml/2½fl oz/⅓ cup cold water to hand. Somen only take 2 minutes to cook. Put the somen in the rapidly boiling water. When it foams again, pour the glass of water in. When the water boils again, the somen are ready. Drain into a colander under cold running water, and rub the somen with your hands to remove the starch. Drain well.

4 Put some ice cubes or a block of ice in the centre of a chilled, large glass bowl, and add the somen. Gently pour on enough ice-cold water to cover the somen, then arrange cucumber slices, prawns and flowers on top.

5 Prepare all the relishes separately in small dishes or small sake cups.

6 Divide approximately one-third of the dipping sauce among four small cups. Put the remaining sauce in a jug (pitcher) or gravy boat.

7 Serve the noodles cold with the relishes. The guests are invited to put any combination of relishes into their dipping-sauce cup. Hold the cup over the somen bowl, pick up a mouthful of somen, then dip them into the sauce and eat. Add more dipping sauce from the jug and more relishes as required.

SAPPORO-STYLE RAMEN NOODLES IN SOUP

THIS IS A RICH AND TANGY SOUP FROM SAPPORO, THE CAPITAL OF HOKKAIDO, WHICH IS JAPAN'S MOST NORTHERLY ISLAND. RAW GRATED GARLIC AND CHILLI OIL ARE ADDED TO WARM THE BODY.

SERVES FOUR

INGREDIENTS
250g/9oz dried ramen noodles
For the soup stock
 4 spring onions (scallions)
 6cm/2½in fresh root ginger, quartered
 raw bones from 2 chickens, washed
 1 large onion, quartered
 4 garlic cloves
 1 large carrot, roughly chopped
 1 egg shell
 120ml/4fl oz/½ cup sake
 90ml/6 tbsp miso (any colour)
 30ml/2 tbsp shoyu
For the toppings
 115g/4oz pork belly
 5cm/2in carrot
 12 mangetouts (snow peas)
 8 baby corn
 15ml/1 tbsp sesame oil
 1 dried red chilli, seeded
  and crushed
 225g/8oz/1 cup beansprouts
 2 spring onions (scallions), chopped
 2 garlic cloves, finely grated
 chilli oil
 salt

1 To make the soup stock, bruise the spring onions and ginger by hitting with a rolling pin. Boil 1.5 litres/2½ pints/6¼ cups water in a heavy pan, add the bones, and cook until the meat changes colour. Discard the water and wash the bones under running water.

2 Wash the pan and boil 2 litres/3½ pints/9 cups water, then add the bones and other stock ingredients except for the miso and shoyu. Reduce the heat to low, and simmer for 2 hours, skimming any scum off. Strain into a bowl through a muslin- (cheesecloth-) lined sieve, this will take about 1–2 hours. Do not squeeze the muslin.

3 Cut the pork into 5mm/¼in slices. Peel and halve the carrot lengthways then cut into 3mm/⅛in thick, 5cm/2in long slices. Boil the carrot, mangetouts and corn for 3 minutes in water. Drain.

4 Heat the sesame oil in a wok and fry the pork slices and chilli. When the colour of the meat has changed, add the beansprouts. Reduce the heat to medium and add 1 litre/1¾ pints/4 cups soup stock. Cook for 5 minutes.

5 Scoop 60ml/4 tbsp soup stock from the wok and mix well with the miso and shoyu in a bowl. Stir back into the soup. Reduce the heat to low.

6 Bring 2 litres/3½ pints/9 cups water to the boil. Cook the noodles until just soft, following the instructions on the packet. Stir constantly. If the water bubbles up, pour in 50ml/2fl oz/¼ cup cold water. Drain well and divide among four bowls.

7 Pour the hot soup on to the noodles and heap the beansprouts and pork on top. Add the carrot, mangetouts and corn. Sprinkle with spring onions and serve with garlic and chilli oil.

TOKYO-STYLE RAMEN NOODLES IN SOUP

RAMEN IS A HYBRID CHINESE NOODLE DISH PRESENTED IN A JAPANESE WAY, AND THERE ARE MANY REGIONAL VARIATIONS FEATURING LOCAL SPECIALITIES. THIS IS A LEGENDARY TOKYO VERSION.

SERVES FOUR

INGREDIENTS
  250g/9oz dried ramen noodles
For the soup stock
  4 spring onions (scallions)
  7.5cm/3in fresh root ginger, quartered
  raw bones from 2 chickens, washed
  1 large onion, quartered
  4 garlic cloves, peeled
  1 large carrot, roughly chopped
  1 egg shell
  120ml/4fl oz/½ cup sake
  about 60ml/4 tbsp shoyu
  2.5ml/½ tsp salt
For the *cha-shu* (pot-roast pork)
  500g/1¼lb pork shoulder, boned
  30ml/2 tbsp vegetable oil
  2 spring onions (scallions), chopped
  2.5cm/1in fresh root ginger, peeled
    and sliced
  15ml/1 tbsp sake
  45ml/3 tbsp shoyu
  15ml/1 tbsp caster (superfine) sugar
For the toppings
  2 hard-boiled eggs
  150g/5oz menma, soaked for
    30 minutes and drained
  ½ nori sheet, broken into pieces
  2 spring onions (scallions), chopped
  ground white pepper
  sesame oil or chilli oil

1 To make the soup stock, bruise the spring onions and ginger by hitting with the side of a large knife or a rolling pin. Pour 1.5 litres/2½ pints/6¼ cups water into a wok and bring to the boil. Add the chicken bones and boil until the colour of the meat changes. Discard the water and wash the bones under water.

2 Wash the wok, bring another 2 litres/3½ pints/9 cups water to the boil and add the bones and the other soup stock ingredients, except for the shoyu and salt. Reduce the heat to low, and simmer until the water has reduced by half, skimming off any scum. Strain into a bowl through a muslin- (cheesecloth-) lined sieve. This will take 1–2 hours.

3 Make the *cha-shu*. Roll the meat up tightly, 8cm/3½in in diameter, and tie it with kitchen string.

4 Wash the wok and dry over a high heat. Heat the oil to smoking point in the wok and add the chopped spring onions and ginger. Cook briefly, then add the meat. Turn often to brown the outside evenly.

5 Sprinkle with sake and add 400ml/14fl oz/1⅔ cups water, the shoyu and sugar. Boil, then reduce the heat to low and cover. Cook for 25–30 minutes, turning every 5 minutes. Remove from the heat.

6 Slice the pork into 12 fine slices. Use any leftover pork for another recipe.

7 Shell and halve the boiled eggs, and sprinkle some salt on to the yolks.

8 Pour 1 litre/1¾ pints/4 cups soup stock from the bowl into a large pan. Boil and add the shoyu and salt. Check the seasoning; add more shoyu if required.

9 Wash the wok again and bring 2 litres/3½ pints/9 cups water to the boil. Cook the ramen noodles according to the packet instructions until just soft. Stir constantly to prevent sticking. If the water bubbles up, pour in 50ml/2fl oz/¼ cup cold water. Drain well and divide among four bowls.

10 Pour the soup over the noodles to cover. Arrange half a boiled egg, pork slices, menma and nori on top, and sprinkle with spring onions. Serve with pepper and sesame or chilli oil. Season to taste with a little salt, if you like.

VEGETABLES
AND SEAWEED

Creating a harmonious effect from seasonal harvests has been

a guiding spirit in Japanese cooking for centuries. Japanese

vegetable dishes are also nutritious and low in fat. In this

chapter there are inspiring combinations of vegetables,

mushrooms and seaweed that are typical of Japanese cooking.

SLOW-COOKED DAIKON

FRESHLY DUG DAIKON IS VERY JUICY, AND IT IS PRAISED AS THE KING OF WINTER VEGETABLES IN JAPAN. IN THIS DISH, KNOWN AS FURO FUKI DAIKON, THE DAIKON IS COOKED SLOWLY AND SERVED WITH TANGY MISO SAUCE. THE RICE ABSORBS THE BITTER JUICES, AND IS THEN DISCARDED.

SERVES FOUR

INGREDIENTS

1kg/2¼lb daikon, cut into 4 × 5cm/
  2in thick discs
15ml/1 tbsp rice (any kind except
  fragrant Thai or basmati)
100ml/3fl oz/scant ½ cup
  hatcho miso
60ml/4 tbsp caster (superfine) sugar
120ml/4fl oz/½ cup mirin
20cm/8in square dried konbu
rind of ¼ yuzu, shaved with a zester,
  to serve (optional)

1 Peel the skin from the daikon and shave the top and bottom edge of each section. Plunge into a bowl of cold water. Drain and place flat in a pan.

2 Pour in enough cold water to come 3cm/1¼in above the daikon. Add the rice and put on a high heat. When it comes to the boil, lower the heat and cook for a further 30 minutes.

3 Meanwhile, mix the miso and sugar in a pan and add the mirin, a tablespoonful at a time, to loosen the mixture. Over a medium heat, heat the miso mixture, stirring continuously. When the mixture thickens, turn the heat to very low. Cook, stirring, until the miso sauce is thick enough to stick to a spoon when you lift it from the pan. Remove from the heat and keep warm.

4 When the daikon is cooked (to test, insert a cocktail stick (toothpick): it should go in easily), gently scoop the daikon discs, one by one, on to a flat-bottomed sieve or a plate. Rinse each disc with water, to remove all the bitter juices. Discard the water and rice in the pan and wash the pan thoroughly.

5 Wipe the konbu with a wet cloth, and place in the bottom of the cleaned pan. Replace the daikon and pour in enough water to just cover. Over a very low heat, warm the daikon for 15 minutes to absorb the flavour of the konbu.

6 Place the daikon in individual bowls. Scoop out a little at the top, if you wish, then pour 15–20ml/3–4 tsp of the miso mixture on each piece and serve garnished with yuzu strips, if using. Serve with a spoon and eat it as you would a dessert.

LIGHTLY BOILED SPINACH WITH TOASTED SESAME SEEDS

O-HITASHI HAS BEEN SERVED AS A SIDE DISH ON JAPANESE DINING TABLES FOR CENTURIES. SEASONAL GREEN VEGETABLES ARE SIMPLY BLANCHED AND COOLED AND FORMED INTO LITTLE TOWERS. WITH A LITTLE HELP FROM SOY SAUCE AND SESAME SEEDS, THEY REVEAL THEIR TRUE FLAVOUR.

2 Drain immediately and place the spinach under running water. Squeeze out all the excess water by hand. Now what looked like a large amount of spinach has become a ball, roughly the size of an orange. Mix the shoyu and water, then pour on to the spinach. Mix well and leave to cool.

3 Meanwhile, put the sesame seeds in a dry frying pan and stir or toss until they start to pop. Remove from the heat and leave to cool.

4 Drain the spinach and squeeze out the excess sauce with your hands. Line up the spinach in the same direction on a chopping board, then form it into a log shape of about 4cm/1½in in diameter. Squeeze again to make it firm. With a sharp knife, cut it across into four cylinders.

SERVES FOUR

INGREDIENTS
    450g/1lb fresh spinach
    30ml/2 tbsp shoyu
    30ml/2 tbsp water
    15ml/1 tbsp sesame seeds
    salt

COOK'S TIP
Japanese spinach, the long-leaf type with the stalks and pink root intact, is best, but you can use ordinary young spinach leaves, or any soft and deep-green salad vegetables – such as watercress, rocket (arugula), lamb's lettuce – instead of the spinach, if you wish.

1 Blanch young spinach leaves in lightly salted boiling water for 15 seconds. For Japanese-type spinach, hold the leafy part and slip the stems into the pan. After 15 seconds, drop in the leaves and cook for 20 seconds.

5 Place the spinach cylinders on a large plate or individual dishes. Sprinkle with the toasted sesame seeds and a little salt, to taste, and serve.

DAIKON AND CARROT SALAD

THIS DISH, CALLED NAMASU IN JAPAN, IS ESSENTIAL FOR THE NEW YEAR'S CELEBRATION MEAL. THE BRIGHT COLOUR COMBINATION OF WHITE DAIKON AND RED CARROT IS PARTICULARLY FAVOURED BY MANY JAPANESE AS IT IS REGARDED AS A SYMBOL OF HAPPINESS. START PREPARATIONS FOR THIS RECIPE THE DAY BEFORE IT IS TO BE EATEN.

SERVES FOUR

INGREDIENTS
20cm/8in daikon
2 carrots
5ml/1 tsp salt
45ml/3 tbsp caster (superfine) sugar
70ml/4½ tbsp rice vinegar
15ml/1 tbsp sesame seeds

COOK'S TIP
This salad can be served with halved hard-boiled eggs, the yolk seasoned with a little mayonnaise and shoyu, and accompanied by sticks of cucumber rolled in smoked salmon. Offer a tiny cup of warm sake to drink with it.

1 Cut the daikon into three pieces, then thickly peel the skin. Peel the carrots and cut them into 5cm/2in pieces. Slice both vegetables very thinly lengthways then crossways to make very thin matchsticks. Alternatively, shred them with a grater or use a mandolin to achieve a similar effect.

2 Place the daikon and carrot in a mixing bowl. Sprinkle with the salt and mix well with your hands. Leave for about 30 minutes. Drain the vegetables in a sieve and gently squeeze out the excess liquid, then transfer them to another mixing bowl.

3 Mix the sugar and rice vinegar together in a bowl. Stir well until the sugar has completely dissolved. Pour over the daikon and carrot, and leave for at least a day, mixing at least two to three times.

4 To serve, mix the two vegetables evenly and heap in the middle of a small bowl or a plate. Sprinkle with sesame seeds and serve.

SPINACH WITH PEANUT SAUCE

TRADITIONAL JAPANESE COOKING RARELY USES FAT OR OIL, AND NUTS HAVE LONG BEEN AN IMPORTANT SOURCE OF ESSENTIAL NUTRITIONAL OILS IN THE JAPANESE DIET. IN THIS RECIPE, CALLED HORENSO PEANUTS AÉ, PEANUTS ARE TRANSFORMED INTO A CREAMY SAUCE AND MIXED WITH SPINACH.

SERVES FOUR

INGREDIENTS
450g/1lb spinach
For the peanut sauce
50g/2oz/⅓ cup unsalted
shelled peanuts
30ml/2 tbsp shoyu
7.5ml/1½ tsp caster (superfine) sugar
25ml/1½ tbsp second dashi stock,
or the same amount of warm water
with a pinch of dashi-no-moto

VARIATIONS
• You can use walnuts or sesame seeds to make different types of sauce.
• Young nettle leaves and coriander (cilantro), blanched and mixed with the peanut sauce, make an interesting "not quite Japanese" dish.

1 First, make the peanut sauce. Grind the shelled peanuts in a suribachi or a mortar and pestle. Alternatively, use an electric grinder.

2 Transfer the crushed nuts to a small mixing bowl and stir in the shoyu, sugar and dashi stock. When thoroughly mixed, the sauce will look like runny peanut butter.

3 Blanch the spinach for 30 seconds in rapidly boiling water until the leaves are wilted. Drain and cool under running water for 30 seconds.

4 Drain again and lightly squeeze out the excess water. Add the peanut sauce to the spinach in a bowl and mix gently but thoroughly. Serve on individual plates or small bowls.

BRAISED TURNIP WITH PRAWN AND MANGETOUT

TAKI-AWASE IS AN ELEGANT DISH IN WHICH THREE COLOURS — THE PINK OF THE PRAWNS, THE WHITE OF THE TURNIPS AND THE GREEN OF THE MANGETOUTS — RESEMBLE A LADY'S SPRING KIMONO.

SERVES FOUR

INGREDIENTS

8 small turnips, peeled
600ml/1 pint/2½ cups second dashi
    stock, or the same amount of water
    and 7.5ml/1½ tsp dashi-no-moto
10ml/2 tsp shoyu (use the Japanese
    pale awakuchi soy sauce
    if available)
60ml/4 tbsp mirin
30ml/2 tbsp sake
16 medium raw tiger prawns (jumbo
    shrimp), heads and shells removed
    with tails intact
dash of rice vinegar
90g/3½oz mangetouts (snow peas)
5ml/1 tsp cornflour (cornstarch)
salt

1 Par-boil the turnips in boiling water for 3 minutes. Drain, then place them side by side in a deep pan. Add the dashi stock and cover with a saucer to submerge the turnips. Bring to the boil, then add the shoyu, 5ml/1 tsp salt, the mirin and sake. Reduce the heat to very low, cover and simmer for 30 minutes.

2 Insert a cocktail stick (toothpick) into the back of each prawn, and gently scoop up the thin black vein running down its length. Very carefully pull the vein out, then discard.

3 Blanch the prawns in boiling water with the vinegar until the colour just changes. Drain. Cook the mangetouts in lightly salted water for 3 minutes. Drain well, then set aside.

4 Remove the saucer from the turnips and add the cooked prawns to the stock for about 4 minutes to warm through. Scoop out the turnips, drain and place in individual bowls. Transfer the prawns to a small plate.

5 Mix the cornflour with 15ml/1 tbsp water and add to the pan that held the turnips. Increase the heat a little bit and shake the pan gently until the liquid thickens slightly.

6 Place the mangetouts on the turnips and arrange the prawns on top, then pour about 30ml/2 tbsp of the hot liquid from the pan into each bowl. Serve immediately.

KABOCHA SQUASH <u>WITH</u> CHICKEN SAUCE

IN THIS DISH, KNOWN AS KABOCHA TORI-SOBORO KAKE, *THE MILD SWEETNESS OF KABOCHA, SIMILAR TO THAT OF SWEET POTATO, GOES VERY WELL WITH THE RICH MEAT SAUCE.*

SERVES FOUR

INGREDIENTS
   1 kabocha squash, about 500g/1¼lb
   ½ yuzu or lime
   20g/¾oz mangetouts (snow peas)
   salt
For the chicken sauce
   100ml/3fl oz/scant ½ cup water
   30ml/2 tbsp sake
   300g/11oz lean chicken,
     minced (ground)
   60ml/4 tbsp caster (superfine) sugar
   60ml/4 tbsp shoyu
   60ml/4 tbsp mirin

1 Halve the kabocha, then remove the seeds and fibre around the seeds. Halve again to make four wedges. Trim the stalky end of the kabocha wedge.

2 Remove strips of the peel on each of the wedges, cutting off strips length-ways of about 1–2.5cm/½–1in wide. The kabocha wedges will now have green (skin) and yellow (flesh) stripes. This will help preserve the kabocha's most tasty part just beneath the skin, and also allows it to be cooked until soft as well as being decorative.

3 Chop each wedge into large bitesize pieces. Place them side by side in a pan. Pour in enough water to cover, then sprinkle with some salt. Cover and cook for 5 minutes over a medium heat, then lower the heat and simmer for 15 minutes until tender. Test the kabocha by pricking with a skewer. When soft enough, remove from heat, cover and leave for 5 minutes.

4 Slice the yuzu or lime into thin discs, then hollow out the inside of the skin to make rings of peel. Cover with a sheet of clear film (plastic wrap) until needed. Blanch the mangetouts in lightly salted water. Drain and set aside.

5 To make the chicken sauce, bring the water and sake to the boil in a pan. Add the minced chicken, and when the colour of the meat has changed, add the sugar, shoyu and mirin. Stir continuously with a hand whisk until the liquid has almost all evaporated.

6 Pile up the kabocha on a large plate, then pour the hot meat sauce on top. Add the mangetouts and serve, garnished with yuzu or lime rings.

COOK'S TIP
Use tofu for a vegetarian sauce. Wrap in kitchen paper and leave for 30 minutes. Mash with a fork, then add in step 5.

CARROT ᴵᴺ SWEET VINEGAR

IN THIS REFRESHING SIDE DISH, CALLED SAN BAI ZU, *FINE CARROT STRIPS ARE MARINATED IN RICE VINEGAR, SHOYU AND MIRIN. IT MAKES A GOOD ACCOMPANIMENT FOR OILY FOODS SUCH AS* TERIYAKI.

SERVES FOUR

INGREDIENTS
2 large carrots, peeled
5ml/1 tsp salt
30ml/2 tbsp sesame seeds
For the sweet vinegar marinade
75ml/5 tbsp rice vinegar
30ml/2 tbsp shoyu (use the pale
  awakuchi soy sauce if available)
45ml/3 tbsp mirin

COOK'S TIP
This marinade is called *san bai zu*, and is one of the essential basic sauces in Japanese cooking. Dilute the marinade with 15ml/1 tbsp second dashi stock, then add sesame seeds and a few dashes of sesame oil for a very tasty and healthy salad dressing.

1 Cut the carrots into thin matchsticks, 5cm/2in long. Put the carrots and salt into a mixing bowl, and mix well with your hands. After 25 minutes, rinse the wilted carrot in cold water, then drain.

2 In another bowl, mix together the marinade ingredients. Add the carrots, and leave to marinate for 3 hours.

3 Put a small pan on a high heat, add the sesame seeds and toss constantly until the seeds start to pop. Remove from the heat and cool.

4 Chop the sesame seeds with a large, sharp knife on a large chopping board. Place the carrots in a bowl, sprinkle with the sesame seeds and serve cold.

FRIED AUBERGINE ᵂᴵᵀᴴ MISO SAUCE

IN NASU-MISO, *STIR-FRIED AUBERGINE IS COATED IN A RICH MISO SAUCE. MAKE SURE THE OIL IS SMOKING HOT WHEN ADDING THE AUBERGINE PIECES, SO THAT THEY DO NOT ABSORB TOO MUCH OIL.*

SERVES FOUR

INGREDIENTS
2 large aubergines (eggplant)
1–2 dried red chillies
45ml/3 tbsp sake
45ml/3 tbsp mirin
45ml/3 tbsp caster (superfine) sugar
30ml/2 tbsp shoyu
45ml/3 tbsp red miso (use either the
  dark red aka miso or even darker
  hatcho miso)
90ml/6 tbsp sesame oil
salt

VARIATION
Sweet (bell) peppers could also be used for this dish instead of the aubergine. Take 1 red, 1 yellow and 2 green peppers. Remove the seeds and chop them into 1cm/½in strips, then follow the rest of the recipe.

1 Cut the aubergines into bitesize pieces and place in a large colander, sprinkle with some salt and leave for 30 minutes to remove the bitter juices. Squeeze the aubergine pieces by hand. Remove the seeds from the chillies and chop the chillies into thin rings.

2 Mix the sake, mirin, sugar and shoyu in a cup. In a separate bowl, mix the red miso with 45ml/3 tbsp water to make a loose paste.

3 Heat the oil in a large pan and add the chilli. When you see pale smoke rising from the oil, add the aubergine, and, using cooking hashi, stir-fry for about 8 minutes, or until tender. Lower the heat to medium.

4 Add the sake mixture to the pan, and stir for 2–3 minutes. If the sauce starts to burn, lower the heat. Add the miso paste to the pan and cook, stirring, for another 2 minutes. Serve hot.

BROAD BEANS, DAIKON AND SALMON ROE

SORA-MAME NO AE-MONO IS A TYPICAL TSUMAMI BAR SNACK EATEN THROUGHOUT JAPAN. THIS UNUSUAL COMBINATION OF COLOURS, FLAVOURS AND TEXTURES MAKES IT IDEAL COMPANY FOR A REFRESHING GLASS OF COLD SAKE IN THE SUMMER MONTHS.

SERVES FOUR

INGREDIENTS
    200g/7oz daikon, peeled
    1 nori sheet
    1kg/2¼lb broad (fava) beans in their
        pods, shelled
    1.5ml/¼ tsp wasabi paste from tube
        or 2.5ml/½ tsp wasabi powder
        mixed with 1.5ml/¼ tsp water
    20ml/4 tsp shoyu
    60ml/4 tbsp ikura
    salt

1 Grate the daikon finely with a daikon grater, or use a food processor to chop it into fine shreds. Place the daikon in a sieve and let the juices drain.

2 Tear the nori with your hands into flakes about 1cm/½in square.

3 In a small pan, cook the broad beans in plenty of rapidly boiling salted water for about 4 minutes. Drain and immediately cool under running water. Remove the skins.

4 Mix the wasabi paste with the shoyu in a small mixing bowl. Add the nori flakes, toasted if you wish, and skinned beans, and mix well.

5 Divide the beans among four individual small bowls, heap on the grated daikon, then spoon the ikura on top. Serve cold. Ask your guests to mix everything well just before eating.

COOK'S TIPS
• The Japanese don't eat the pods of broad beans. When the beans are in season, people buy huge quantities of them. Shelled, unskinned beans are cooked in salted water as salty as sea water, then drained and heaped into a large bowl. You pick one up and snap the top tip off the skins then squeeze the bright green contents into your mouth.
• Toasting the nori sheet gives it a crisp texture and enhances its flavour. Before tearing into small pieces, wave the edge of the nori over a medium gas flame very quickly a few times.

SLOW-COOKED SHIITAKE WITH SHOYU

SHIITAKE COOKED SLOWLY ARE SO RICH AND FILLING, THAT SOME PEOPLE CALL THEM "VEGETARIAN STEAK". THIS DISH, KNOWN AS FUKUMÉ-NI, *CAN LAST A FEW WEEKS IN THE REFRIGERATOR, AND IS A USEFUL AND FLAVOURFUL ADDITION TO OTHER DISHES.*

SERVES FOUR

INGREDIENTS
20 dried shiitake mushrooms
45ml/3 tbsp vegetable oil
30ml/2 tbsp shoyu
25ml/1½ tbsp caster (superfine)
  sugar
15ml/1 tbsp toasted sesame oil

VARIATION
To make shiitake rice, cut the slow-cooked shiitake into thin strips. Mix with 600g/1lb 5oz/5¼ cups cooked rice and 15ml/1 tbsp finely chopped chives. Serve in individual rice bowls and sprinkle with toasted sesame seeds.

1 Start soaking the dried shiitake the day before. Put them in a large bowl almost full of water. Cover the shiitake with a plate or lid to stop them floating to the surface of the water. Leave to soak overnight.

2 Measure 120ml/4fl oz/½ cup liquid from the bowl. Drain the shiitake into a sieve. Remove and discard the stalks.

3 Heat the oil in a wok or a large pan. Stir-fry the shiitake over a high heat for 5 minutes, stirring continuously.

4 Reduce the heat to the lowest setting, then add the measured liquid, the shoyu and sugar. Cook until there is almost no moisture left, stirring frequently. Add the sesame oil and remove from the heat.

5 Leave to cool, then slice and arrange the shiitake on a large plate.

STEAMED AUBERGINE <u>WITH</u> SESAME SAUCE

THIS AUTUMN RECIPE, NASU RIKYU-NI, REPRESENTS A TYPICAL ZEN TEMPLE COOKING STYLE. FRESH SEASONAL VEGETABLES ARE CHOSEN AND COOKED WITH CARE. THIS DISH IS ALSO DELICIOUS COLD.

SERVES FOUR

INGREDIENTS

2 large aubergines (eggplant)
400ml/14fl oz/1⅔ cups second dashi
  stock, or the same amount of water
  with 5ml/1 tsp dashi-no-moto
25ml/1½ tbsp caster (superfine)
  sugar
15ml/1 tbsp shoyu
15ml/1 tbsp sesame seeds, finely
  ground in a suribachi or mortar
  and pestle
15ml/1 tbsp sake
15ml/1 tbsp cornflour (cornstarch)
salt
For the accompanying vegetables
130g/4½oz shimeji mushrooms
115g/4oz/¾ cup fine green beans
100ml/3fl oz/scant ½ cup second
  dashi stock, or the same amount of
  water with 5ml/1 tsp dashi-no-moto
25ml/1½ tbsp caster (superfine)
  sugar
15ml/1 tbsp sake
1.5ml/¼ tsp salt
dash of shoyu

1 Peel the aubergines and cut in quarters lengthways. Prick all over with a skewer, then plunge into salted water for 30 minutes.

2 Drain and steam the aubergines in a steamer, or in a hot wok with a bamboo basket inside, for 20 minutes, or until soft. If the quarters are too long to fit in the steamer, cut in half.

3 Mix the dashi stock, sugar, shoyu and 1.5ml/¼ tsp salt together in a large pan. Gently transfer the aubergines to this pan, then cover and cook over a low heat for a further 15 minutes. Take a few tablespoonfuls of stock from the pan and mix with the ground sesame seeds. Add this mixture to the pan.

4 Thoroughly mix the sake with the cornflour, add to the pan with the aubergines and stock and shake the pan gently, but quickly. When the sauce becomes quite thick, remove the pan from the heat.

5 While the aubergines are cooking, prepare and cook the accompanying vegetables. Wash the mushrooms and cut off the hard base part. Separate the large block into smaller chunks with your fingers. Trim the green beans and cut in half.

6 Mix the stock with the sugar, sake, salt and shoyu in a shallow pan. Add the green beans and mushrooms and cook for 7 minutes until just tender. Serve the aubergines and their sauce in individual bowls with the accompanying vegetables over the top.

NEW POTATOES COOKED IN DASHI STOCK

NIKKOROGASHI IS A SIMPLE YET SCRUMPTIOUS DISH, INVOLVING LITTLE MORE THAN NEW SEASON'S POTATOES AND ONION COOKED IN DASHI STOCK. AS THE STOCK EVAPORATES, THE ONION BECOMES MELTINGLY SOFT AND CARAMELIZED, MAKING A WONDERFUL SAUCE THAT COATS THE POTATOES.

SERVES FOUR

INGREDIENTS

    15ml/1 tbsp toasted sesame oil
    1 small onion, thinly sliced
    1kg/2¼lb baby new potatoes,
      unpeeled
    200ml/7fl oz/scant 1 cup second
      dashi stock, or the same amount of
      water with 5ml/1 tsp dashi-no-moto
    45ml/3 tbsp shoyu

COOK'S TIP
Japanese chefs use toasted sesame oil
for its distinctive strong aroma. If the
smell is too strong, use a mixture of half
sesame and half vegetable oil.

1 Heat the sesame oil in a wok or large
pan. Add the onion slices and stir-fry for
30 seconds, then add the potatoes. Stir
constantly, using cooking hashi for
ease, until all the potatoes are well
coated in sesame oil.

2 Pour on the dashi stock and shoyu
and reduce the heat to the lowest
setting. Cover and cook for 15 minutes,
turning the potatoes every 5 minutes so
that they are evenly cooked.

3 Uncover the wok or pan for a further
5 minutes to reduce the liquid. If there
is already very little liquid remaining,
remove the wok or pan from the heat,
cover and leave to stand for 5 minutes.
Check that the potatoes are cooked,
then remove from the heat.

4 Transfer the potatoes and onions to a
deep serving bowl. Pour the sauce over
the top and serve immediately.

VEGETARIAN TEMPURA

IN THE HOT AND HUMID JAPANESE SUMMER, ZEN MONKS EAT DEEP-FRIED VEGETABLES, SHOJIN-AGÉ, TO GET OVER THE FATIGUE OF HARD TRAINING. ALTHOUGH TEMPURA PREPARATION NEEDS A LITTLE EFFORT, TAKE YOUR TIME AND ENJOY THE PROCESS AS AN ARTISTIC ACTIVITY, LIKE THE MONKS DO.

SERVES FOUR

INGREDIENTS
15ml/1 tbsp lemon juice or
    rice vinegar
15cm/6in renkon
½ sweet potato
½ aubergine (eggplant)
vegetable oil and sesame oil, for
    frying (see Cook's Tips)
4 shiso leaves
1 green (bell) pepper, seeded and cut
    lengthways into 2.5cm/1in wide strips
⅛ kabocha squash, cut into 5mm/¼in
    thick half-ring shapes
4 green beans, trimmed
4 fresh shiitake mushrooms
4 okra, trimmed
1 onion, sliced into 5mm/¼in rings
For the batter
200ml/7fl oz/scant 1 cup ice-
    cold water
1 large (US extra large) egg, beaten
90g/3½oz/generous ¾ cup sifted
    plain (all-purpose) flour, plus extra
    for dusting
2–3 ice cubes
For the condiment
450g/1lb daikon
4cm/1½in piece fresh root ginger
For the dipping sauce
400ml/14fl oz/1⅔ cups second dashi
    stock, or the same amount of water
    with 10ml/2 tsp dashi-no-moto
100ml/3fl oz/scant ½ cup shoyu
100ml/3fl oz/scant ½ cup mirin

1 To make the dipping sauce, mix all the ingredients in a pan. Bring to the boil, then remove from the heat. Set aside.

2 Fill a small bowl with cold water and add the lemon juice or rice vinegar. Peel the renkon, then slice it and the sweet potato into 5mm/¼in thick discs. Plunge the pieces into the bowl straightaway to prevent discolouring. Just before frying, drain and pat dry with kitchen paper.

3 Slice the aubergine horizontally into 5mm/¼in thick slices, then halve them lengthways. Soak in cold water until just before frying. Drain and pat dry.

4 To prepare the condiment, peel and grate the daikon and ginger separately, using a daikon-oroshi, or, alternatively, use a food processor. Lightly squeeze out excess liquid from both the daikon and ginger.

5 Line an egg cup with clear film (plastic wrap) and press about 2.5ml/½ tsp grated ginger into the bottom, then put in 30ml/2 tbsp grated daikon. Press again and turn upside-down on to a small plate. Make four of these tiny mounds.

6 To make the batter, pour the ice-cold water into a mixing bowl, add the beaten egg and mix well. Add the flour and very roughly fold in with a pair of chopsticks or a fork. Do not beat. The batter should still be quite lumpy. Add the ice cubes.

7 Pour in enough oil to come halfway up the depth of a wok or deep-fryer. Heat the oil until the temperature reaches about 150°C/300°F.

8 Deep-fry the shiso leaves. Hold the stalk of one leaf in your hand and stroke the leaf across the surface of the batter mix, coating only one side of the leaf. Gently slip it into the oil until it goes crisp and bright green. Leave to drain on kitchen paper. Deep-fry the renkon and sweet potato in the same way; first coating one side in batter then frying until golden.

9 Increase the temperature to 175°C/347°F. Lightly dust the rest of the vegetables with flour, dunk into the batter mix, then shake off the excess. Deep-fry them two to three pieces at a time until crisp. Leave to drain on kitchen paper.

10 Divide the warm dipping sauce among four small bowls. Place with the condiment. Arrange the tempura on a large plate. Serve immediately. Mix the condiment into the sauce, then dip in the tempura as you eat.

COOK'S TIPS
• If you like the strong flavour of sesame oil, mix it with 2 parts vegetable oil. For a lighter flavour, just add a few dashes of toasted sesame oil to the vegetable oil.
• To check the temperature of oil without a thermometer, drop a little batter into the hot oil. At 150°C/300°F it should sink down to the bottom and stay there for about 5 seconds before it floats to the surface. When the temperature reaches 175°C/347°F, a drop of batter sinks to the bottom, but immediately rises to the surface.

BACON-ROLLED ENOKITAKE MUSHROOMS

THE JAPANESE NAME FOR THIS DISH IS OBIMAKI ENOKI: AN OBI (BELT OR SASH) IS MADE FROM BACON AND WRAPPED AROUND ENOKITAKE MUSHROOMS BEFORE GRILLING THEM. THE STRONG, SMOKY FLAVOUR OF THE BACON ACCOMPANIES THE SUBTLE FLAVOUR OF ENOKI VERY WELL.

SERVES FOUR

INGREDIENTS
    450g/1lb fresh enokitake mushrooms
    6 rindless smoked streaky (fatty)
        bacon rashers (strips)
    4 lemon wedges and ground white
        pepper, to serve

1 Cut off the root part of each enokitake cluster 2cm/¾in from the end. Do not separate the stems. Cut the rashers in half lengthways.

2 Divide the enokitake into 12 bunches. Take one bunch, then place the middle of the enokitake near the edge of 1 bacon rasher. You should be able to see 2.5–4cm/1–1½in of enokitake at each end of the bacon.

3 Carefully roll up the bunch of enokitake in the bacon. Tuck any straying short stems into the bacon and slide the bacon slightly upwards at each roll to cover about 4cm/1½in of the enokitake. Secure the end of the bacon roll with a cocktail stick (toothpick). Repeat using the remaining enokitake and bacon to make 11 more rolls.

4 Preheat the grill (broiler) to high. Place the enokitake rolls on an oiled wire rack. Grill (broil) both sides until the bacon is crisp and the enokitake start to burn. This takes about 10–13 minutes.

5 Remove the enokitake rolls and place on a board. Using a fork and knife, chop each roll in half in the middle of the bacon belt. Arrange the top part of the enokitake roll standing upright, the bottom part lying down next to it. Serve with a wedge of lemon and a small heap of ground white pepper.

VARIATIONS
A bunch of chives can be rolled and cooked in the same way. You can also use young garlic shoots when they are about 12cm/4½in long for this recipe.

HIJIKI SEAWEED AND CHICKEN

THE TASTE OF HIJIKI IS SOMEWHERE BETWEEN RICE AND VEGETABLE. IT GOES WELL WITH MEAT OR TOFU PRODUCTS, ESPECIALLY WHEN IT'S STIR-FRIED WITH A LITTLE OIL FIRST.

SERVES FOUR

INGREDIENTS
  90g/3½oz dried hijiki seaweed
  150g/5oz chicken breast portion
    with skin
  ½ small carrot, about 5cm/2in
  15ml/1 tbsp vegetable oil
  100ml/3fl oz/scant ½ cup second
    dashi stock, or the same amount of
    water plus 1.5ml/¼ tsp dashi-no-moto
  30ml/2 tbsp sake
  30ml/2 tbsp caster (superfine) sugar
  45ml/3 tbsp shoyu
  a pinch of shichimi togarashi or
    cayenne pepper

1 Soak the hijiki in cold water for about 30 minutes. When ready to cook, it is easily crushed between the fingers. Pour into a sieve and wash under running water. Drain.

2 Peel the skin from the chicken and par-boil the skin in rapidly boiling water for 1 minute, then drain. With a sharp knife, shave off all the yellow fat from the skin. Discard the clear membrane between the fat and the skin as well. Cut the skin into thin strips about 5mm/¼in wide and 2.5cm/1in long. Cut the meat into small, bitesize chunks.

3 Peel and chop the carrot into long, narrow matchsticks.

4 Heat the oil in a wok or frying pan and stir-fry the strips of chicken skin for 5 minutes, or until golden and curled up. Add the chicken meat and keep stirring until the colour changes.

5 Add the hijiki and carrot, then stir-fry for a further minute. Add the remaining ingredients. Lower the heat and cook for 5 minutes.

6 Remove the pan from the heat and leave to stand for about 10 minutes. Serve in small individual bowls. Sprinkle with shichimi togarashi, or cayenne pepper, if preferred.

COOK'S TIP
Chicken skin is unpopular today because of its high calorie content. However, in this dish the thick yellow fat is removed from the skin before cooking, thus greatly reducing the fat content.

DEEP-FRIED LAYERED SHIITAKE AND SCALLOPS

IN THIS DISH, YOU CAN TASTE THREE KINDS OF SOFTNESS: CHEWY SHIITAKE, MASHED NAGA-IMO WITH MISO, AND SUCCULENT SCALLOP. THE MIXTURE CREATES A MOMENT OF HEAVEN IN YOUR MOUTH. IF IT'S DIFFICULT TO EAT WITH CHOPSTICKS, FEEL FREE TO USE A KNIFE AND FORK!

SERVES FOUR

INGREDIENTS
4 scallops
8 large fresh shiitake mushrooms
225g/8oz naga-imo, unpeeled
20ml/4 tsp miso
50g/2oz/1 cup fresh breadcrumbs
cornflour (cornstarch), for dusting
vegetable oil, for deep-frying
2 eggs, beaten
salt
4 lemon wedges, to serve

1 Slice the scallops in two horizontally, then sprinkle with salt. Remove the stalks from the shiitake by cutting them off with a knife. Discard the stalks.

2 Cut shallow slits on the top of the shiitake to form a "hache" symbol or cut slits to form a white cross. Sprinkle with a little salt.

3 Heat a steamer and steam the naga-imo for 10–15 minutes, or until soft. Test with a skewer. Leave to cool.

4 Wait until the naga-imo is cool enough to handle. Skin, then mash the flesh in a bowl with a masher, getting rid of any lumps. Add the miso and mix well. Take the breadcrumbs into your hands and break them down finely. Mix half into the mashed naga-imo, keeping the rest on a small plate.

5 Fill the underneath of the shiitake caps with a scoop of mashed naga-imo. Smooth down with the flat edge of a knife and dust the mash with cornflour.

6 Add a little mash to a slice of scallop and place on top.

7 Spread another 5ml/1 tsp mashed naga-imo on to the scallop and shape to completely cover. Make sure all the ingredients are clinging together. Repeat to make eight little mounds.

8 Heat the oil to 150°C/300°F. Place the beaten eggs in a shallow container. Dust the shiitake and scallop mounds with cornflour, then dip into the egg. Handle with care as the mash and scallop are quite soft. Coat well with the remaining breadcrumbs and deep-fry in the oil until golden. Drain well on kitchen paper. Serve hot on individual plates with a wedge of lemon.

VARIATION
For a vegetarian option, use 16 shiitake mushrooms. Sandwich the naga-imo mash between two shiitake to make 8 bundles. Deep-fry in the same way as the scallop version.

COOK'S TIPS
• Fresh naga-imo produces a slimy liquid when it's cut. Try not to touch this as some people can react and develop a mild rash. When it's cooked, it is perfectly safe to touch.
• If you can't find naga-imo, use yam or 115g/4oz each of potatoes and peeled Jerusalem artichokes instead. Steam the potatoes and boil the artichokes until both are tender.

WAKAME WITH PRAWNS AND CUCUMBER IN VINEGAR DRESSING

THIS SALAD-STYLE DISH, CALLED SUNO-MONO, USES WAKAME SEAWEED, WHICH IS RICH IN MINERALS AND B COMPLEX VITAMINS AND VITAMIN C — SAID TO MAKE YOUR HAIR LOOK SHINY.

2 Peel the prawns, including the tails. Insert a cocktail stick (toothpick) into the back of each prawn and gently scoop up the thin black vein running down its length. Pull it out, then discard.

3 Boil the prawns in lightly salted water until they curl up completely to make full circles. Drain and cool.

4 Halve the cucumber lengthways. Peel away half of the green skin with a zester or vegetable peeler to create green and white stripes. Scoop out the centre with a tablespoon. Slice very thinly with a sharp knife or a mandolin. Sprinkle with 5ml/1 tsp salt, and leave for 15 minutes in a sieve.

5 Blanch the wakame very briefly in boiling water. Drain and cool under cold running water. Add to the cucumber in the sieve. Press the cucumber and wakame to remove the excess liquid. Repeat this two to three times.

6 Mix the dressing ingredients in a mixing bowl. Stir well until the sugar has dissolved. Add the wakame and cucumber to the dressing and mix.

7 Pile up in four small bowls. Lean the prawns against the heap. Garnish with ginger.

SERVES FOUR

INGREDIENTS
  10g/¼oz dried wakame
  12 medium raw tiger prawns
    (jumbo shrimp), heads removed
    but tails intact
  ½ cucumber
  salt
For the dressing
  60ml/4 tbsp rice vinegar
  15ml/1 tbsp shoyu
  7.5ml/1½ tsp caster (superfine) sugar
  2.5cm/1in fresh root ginger, peeled
    and cut into thin strips, to garnish

1 Soak the wakame in a pan or bowl of cold water for 15 minutes until fully open. The wakame expands by three to five times its original size. Drain.

VARIATION
For a vegetarian version, omit the shellfish and add a handful of toasted pine nuts.

ASSORTED SEAWEED SALAD

KAISOU SALADA IS A FINE EXAMPLE OF THE TRADITIONAL JAPANESE IDEA OF EATING: LOOK AFTER YOUR APPETITE AND YOUR HEALTH AT THE SAME TIME. SEAWEED IS A NUTRITIOUS, ALKALINE FOOD AND RICH IN FIBRE. MOREOVER, IT HAS VIRTUALLY NO CALORIES!

SERVES FOUR

INGREDIENTS
  5g/⅛oz each dried wakame, dried
    arame and dried hijiki seaweeds
  about 130g/4½oz enokitake
    mushrooms
  2 spring onions (scallions)
  a few ice cubes
  ½ cucumber, cut lengthways
  250g/9oz mixed salad leaves
For the marinade
  15ml/1 tbsp rice vinegar
  6.5ml/1¼ tsp salt
For the dressing
  60ml/4 tbsp rice vinegar
  7.5ml/1½ tsp toasted sesame oil
  15ml/1 tbsp shoyu
  15ml/1 tbsp second dashi stock, or
    the same amount of water with a
    pinch of dashi-no-moto
  2.5cm/1in piece fresh root ginger,
    finely grated

1 Soak the wakame for 10 minutes in one bowl of water and, in a separate bowl of water, soak the arame and hijiki for 30 minutes together.

2 Trim the hard end of the enokitake stalks, then cut the bunch in half and separate the stems.

3 Cut the spring onions into thin, 4cm/1½in long strips, then soak the strips in cold water with a few ice cubes to make them curl up. Drain. Slice the cucumber into thin, half-moon shapes.

4 Cook the wakame and enokitake in boiling water for 2 minutes, then add the arame and hijiki for a few seconds. Immediately remove from the heat. Drain and sprinkle over the vinegar and salt while still warm. Chill.

5 Mix the dressing ingredients in a bowl. Arrange the mixed salad leaves in a large bowl with the cucumber on top, then add the seaweed and enokitake mixture. Decorate with spring onion strips and serve with the dressing.

DAIKON LAYERED WITH SMOKED SALMON

THE ORIGINAL RECIPE CALLS FOR LAYERED, SALTED SLICED SALMON AND DAIKON, PICKLED IN A WOODEN BARREL FOR A LONG TIME. THIS MODERN VERSION IS LESS SALTY AND FAR EASIER TO MAKE.

SERVES FOUR

INGREDIENTS
  10cm/4in daikon, about 6cm/2½in
    in diameter, peeled
  10ml/2 tsp salt
  5ml/1 tsp rice vinegar
  5cm/2in square dashi-konbu,
    chopped into 1cm/½in strips
  50g/2oz smoked salmon,
    thinly sliced
  2.5ml/½ tsp white poppy seeds

COOK'S TIPS
• You can use a mandolin, a food cutter or a vegetable slicer to make paper-thin slices of daikon.
• If unsure, taste the daikon after salting and squeezing to check whether it needs to be rinsed. The degree of saltiness will depend on the original water content of the daikon.

1 Slice the daikon very thinly into rounds. Put in a shallow container, sprinkle with salt and vinegar, and add the snipped dashi-konbu. Mix and rub gently with the hands. Cover and leave in the refrigerator for 1 hour.

2 Drain in a sieve and squeeze out the excess liquid. If necessary, rinse with running water for 30 seconds, then drain and squeeze out again.

3 Cut the smoked salmon slices into 4cm/1½in squares. Take 1 slice of daikon, top with a salmon slice, then cover with another daikon slice. Repeat until all the salmon is used. Place in a shallow container, cover, then leave to pickle at room temperature for up to 1 day.

4 Arrange the daikon rounds on a serving plate and put a pinch of poppy seeds in the centre.

BROCCOLI AND CUCUMBER PICKLED IN MISO

BROCCOLI STEM IS USUALLY WASTED BECAUSE OF THE FIBROUS TEXTURE, BUT YOU WILL BE SURPRISED HOW TASTY IT IS WHEN MARINATED OR PICKLED. IN YASAI MISO ZUKE, MISO AND GARLIC GIVE A KICK TO ITS SUBTLE FLAVOUR. THIS MAKES A GOOD ACCOMPANIMENT TO DRINKS.

SERVES FOUR

INGREDIENTS
  3 broccoli stems (use the florets in
    another dish, if you wish)
  2 Japanese or salad cucumbers,
    ends trimmed
  200ml/7fl oz/scant 1 cup miso
    (any kind)
  15ml/1 tbsp sake
  1 garlic clove, crushed

1 Peel the broccoli stems and quarter them lengthways.

2 With a vegetable peeler, peel the cucumber every 5mm/¼in to make green-and-white stripes. Cut in half lengthways. Scoop out the centre with a teaspoon. Cut into 7.5cm/3in lengths.

3 Mix the miso, sake and crushed garlic in a deep, plastic or metal container with a lid. Remove half the miso mix.

4 Lay some of the broccoli stems and cucumber flat in the container and push into the miso mix. Spread a little of the reserved miso over the top of the broccoli and cucumber as well.

5 Repeat this process to make a few layers of vegetables and miso, filling up the container. Cover with the lid and leave in the refrigerator for 1–5 days.

6 Take out the vegetables, wash off the miso under running water, then wipe with kitchen paper. Cut the broccoli stem pieces in half then slice into thin strips lengthways. Cut the cucumber into 5mm/¼in thick half-moon slices. Serve cold.

VARIATION
Carrot, turnip, kohlrabi, celery, radish or thinly sliced cabbage stems can be used in this way. The garlic can be replaced by ginger, chilli or lime rind.

BEANS, TOFU
AND EGGS

The virtues of tofu as a nutrient could fill a book,

and the uses of this wonder food are limitless. Its essential

blandness adapts to and absorbs a host of other flavours.

Beans and eggs are equally as versatile and are perfect for

making even the simplest of dishes healthy and filling.

SWEET AZUKI BEAN SOUP WITH MOCHI RICE CAKE

AZUKI BEANS ARE COMMONLY USED IN TRADITIONAL JAPANESE DESSERTS. THIS SWEET SOUP FOR WINTER IS EATEN BETWEEN MEALS AS A SNACK, BUT NEVER AFTER THE MEAL AS IT IS QUITE FILLING.

SERVES FOUR

INGREDIENTS
  130g/4½oz/⅔ cup dried azuki beans
  pinch of baking powder
  130g/4½oz/scant ¾ cup caster
    (superfine) sugar
  1.5ml/¼ tsp salt
  4 mochi

1 Soak the azuki beans overnight in 1 litre/1¾ pints/4 cups water.

2 Pour the beans and the soaking water into a heavy large pan, then bring to the boil. Reduce the heat to medium-low and add the baking powder. Cover the pan and cook for about 30 minutes. Add a further 1 litre/1¾ pints/4 cups water, and bring back to the boil. Reduce the heat to low, and cook for a further 30 minutes.

3 To test that the beans are ready, pick out and press one bean between the fingers. It should crush without any effort. If it is still hard, cook for another 15–20 minutes, then check again.

4 Divide the sugar into two equal heaps. Add one heap to the pan containing the beans and stir gently. Cook for about 3 minutes, then add the rest and wait for another 3 minutes.

5 Add the salt and cook for another 3 minutes. The soup is now ready to eat. Reduce the heat and keep warm.

6 Cut the mochi in half. Grill (broil) under a moderate heat until light golden brown and puffy. Turn several times.

7 Put 2 pieces of mochi into small soup or Japanese wooden bowls and pour the soup around them. Serve hot, and eat with a ceramic or wooden spoon.

COOK'S TIP
This is an easy method for busy people to cook azuki. Soak the beans overnight. Next morning, empty the beans and liquid into a pan and bring to the boil. Transfer the beans and liquid to a vacuum flask. Seal and leave until the evening, ready for adding the sugar in step 4.

COOKED BLACK-EYED BEANS

TRADITIONALLY, THIS DISH WAS SERVED IN THE COLDEST TIME OF THE YEAR USING ONLY PRESERVED FOOD SUCH AS SALTED SALMON AND DRIED VEGETABLES. HERE, FRESH SALMON AND VEGETABLES ARE USED INSTEAD. IT KEEPS FOR 4–5 DAYS IN A COOL PLACE.

SERVES FOUR

INGREDIENTS

150g/5oz salmon fillet, boned and skinned
400g/14oz can black-eyed beans (peas) in brine
50g/2oz fresh shiitake mushrooms, stalks removed
50g/2oz carrot, peeled
50g/2oz daikon, peeled
5g/⅛oz dashi-konbu about 10cm/ 4in square
60ml/4 tbsp water
5ml/1 tsp caster (superfine) sugar
15ml/1 tbsp shoyu
7.5ml/1½ tsp mirin
salt
2.5cm/1in fresh root ginger, peeled and thinly sliced or grated, to garnish

1 Slice the salmon into 1cm/½in thick pieces. Thoroughly salt the fillet and leave for 1 hour, then wash away the salt and cut it into 1cm/½in cubes. Par-boil in rapidly boiling water in a small pan for 30 seconds, then drain. Gently wash under running water.

2 Slice the fresh ginger thinly lengthways, then stack the slices and cut into thin threads. Soak in cold water for 30 minutes, then drain well.

3 Drain the can of beans and tip the liquid into a medium pan. Set the beans and liquid aside.

4 Chop all the vegetables into 1cm/½in cubes. Wipe the dried konbu with a damp dishtowel or kitchen paper, then snip with scissors.

5 Add the salmon, vegetables and konbu to the bean liquid with the beans, water, sugar and 1.5ml/¼ tsp salt. Bring to the boil. Reduce the heat to low and cook for 6 minutes or until the carrot is cooked. Add the shoyu and cook for 4 minutes. Add the mirin, then remove the pan from the heat, mix well and check the seasoning. Leave for an hour. Serve garnished with the ginger.

PAN-FRIED TOFU WITH CARAMELIZED SAUCE

TOFU IN THE WEST IS OFTEN USED AS A MEAT SUBSTITUTE FOR VEGETARIANS, AS IT WAS BY CHINESE BUDDHIST MONKS WHO FIRST BROUGHT VEGETARIAN COOKING INTO JAPAN. THEY INVENTED MANY DELICIOUS AND FILLING PROTEIN DISHES FROM TOFU AND OTHER SOYA BEAN PRODUCTS. THIS DISH IS A MODERN ADDITION TO THAT TRADITION.

SERVES FOUR

INGREDIENTS
    2 × 285g/10¼oz packets tofu blocks
    4 garlic cloves
    10ml/2 tsp vegetable oil
    50g/2oz/¼ cup butter, cut into
      5 equal pieces
    watercress, to garnish
For the marinade
    4 spring onions (scallions)
    60ml/4 tbsp sake
    60ml/4 tbsp shoyu (tamari or sashimi
      soy sauce, if available)
    60ml/4 tbsp mirin

1 Unpack the tofu blocks and discard the liquid, then wrap in three layers of kitchen paper. Put a large plate or wooden chopping board on top as a weight and leave for 30 minutes to allow time for the excess liquid to be absorbed by the paper. This process makes the tofu firmer and, when cooked, it will crisp on the outside.

2 To make the marinade, chop the spring onions finely. Mix with the other marinade ingredients in a ceramic or aluminium tray with sides or a wide, shallow bowl. Leave for 15 minutes.

3 Slice the garlic very thinly to make garlic chips. Heat the vegetable oil in a frying pan and fry the garlic for a few moments until golden. Turn the chips frequently to prevent sticking and burning. Scoop them out on to kitchen paper. Reserve the oil in the pan.

4 Unwrap the tofu. Slice one block horizontally in half, then cut each half into four pieces. Repeat with the other tofu block. Soak in the marinade for about 15 minutes.

5 Take out the tofu and wipe off the excess marinade with kitchen paper. Reserve the marinade.

6 Reheat the oil in the frying pan and add one piece of butter. When the oil starts sizzling, reduce the heat to medium and add the pieces of tofu one by one. Cook in one layer, if possible.

7 Cover the pan and cook until the edge of the tofu is browned and quite firm, approximately 5–8 minutes on each side. (If the edges burn but the centre is pale, reduce the heat.)

8 Pour the marinade into the pan. Cook for 2 minutes, or until the spring onion is very soft. Remove the tofu and arrange four pieces on each serving plate. Pour the thickened marinade and spring onion mixture over the tofu and top with a piece of butter. Sprinkle with the garlic chips and garnish with watercress. Serve hot.

DEEP-FRIED TOFU BALLS

THERE ARE MANY VARIATIONS OF THESE DELICIOUS DEEP-FRIED TOFU BALLS CALLED HIRYOZU, *MEANING FLYING DRAGON'S HEAD. THIS IS ONE OF THE EASIEST TO MAKE.*

MAKES SIXTEEN

INGREDIENTS

2 × 285g/10¼oz packets tofu blocks
20g/¾oz carrot, peeled
40g/1½oz/1¼ cups green beans
2 large (US extra large) eggs, beaten
30ml/2 tbsp sake
10ml/2 tsp mirin
5ml/1 tsp salt
10ml/2 tsp shoyu
pinch of caster (superfine) sugar
vegetable oil, for deep-frying
For the lime sauce
45ml/3 tbsp shoyu
juice of ½ lime
5ml/1 tsp rice vinegar
For the garnish
300g/11oz daikon, peeled
2 dried red chillies, halved
and seeded
4 chives, finely snipped

1 Drain the tofu and wrap in a clean dishtowel or some kitchen paper. Set a chopping board, or large plate with a weight, on top and leave for 2 hours, or until the tofu loses most of its liquid and its weight is halved.

2 Cut the daikon for the garnish into about 4cm/1½in thick slices. Make 3–4 holes in each slice with a skewer or chopstick and insert chilli pieces into the holes. Leave for 15 minutes, then grate the daikon and chilli finely.

3 To make the tofu balls, chop the carrot finely. Trim and cut the beans into 5mm/¼in lengths. Cook both vegetables for 1 minute in boiling water.

4 In a food processor, mix the tofu, eggs, sake, mirin, salt, shoyu and sugar until smooth. Transfer to a bowl and mix in the carrot and beans.

5 Fill a wok or pan with oil 4cm/1½in deep, and heat to 185°C/365°F.

6 Soak a piece of kitchen paper with a little vegetable oil, and wet your hands with it. Scoop 40ml/2½ tbsp tofu mixture in one hand and shape into a ball by tossing the ball between your hands.

7 Carefully slide into the oil and deep-fry until crisp and golden brown. Drain on kitchen paper. Repeat with the remaining mixture.

8 Arrange the tofu balls on a serving plate and sprinkle with chives. Put 30ml/2 tbsp grated daikon in each of four small bowls. Mix the lime sauce ingredients in a serving bowl. Serve the balls with the lime sauce to be mixed with grated daikon by each guest.

SIMMERED TOFU WITH VEGETABLES

A TYPICAL JAPANESE DINNER AT HOME CONSISTS OF A SOUP, THREE DIFFERENT DISHES AND A BOWL OF RICE. ONE OF THE THREE DISHES IS ALWAYS A SIMMERED ONE LIKE THIS.

SERVES FOUR

INGREDIENTS

4 dried shiitake mushrooms
450g/1lb daikon
2 atsu-age, about 200g/7oz each
115g/4oz/¾ cup green beans,
    trimmed and cut in half
5ml/1 tsp rice (any except for
    fragrant Thai or white basmati)
115g/4oz carrot, peeled and cut into
    1cm/½in thick slices
300g/11oz baby potatoes, unpeeled
750ml/1¼ pints/3 cups second dashi
    stock, or the same amount of water
    and 7.5ml/1½ tsp dashi-no-moto
30ml/2 tbsp caster (superfine) sugar
75ml/5 tbsp shoyu
45ml/3 tbsp sake
15ml/1 tbsp mirin

1 Soak the dried shiitake in 250ml/
8fl oz/1 cup water for 2 hours. Drain
and discard the liquid. Remove and
discard the stalks.

2 Peel the daikon and slice into
1cm/½in discs. Shave the edge of the
daikon discs to ensure they are evenly
cooked. Plunge into cold water.

3 Put the atsu-age in a sieve, and wash
off the excess oil with hot water from
the kettle. Drain and cut into pieces of
about 2.5 × 5cm/1 × 2in.

4 Boil the green beans for 2 minutes
and then drain them, cooling them
under running water.

5 Cover the daikon with water in a pan
and add the rice. Bring to the boil then
reduce the heat to medium-low. Cook
for 15 minutes, then drain. Discard
the rice.

6 Put the atsu-age and the mushrooms,
carrot and potatoes into the pan with
the daikon. Add the dashi stock, bring
to the boil, then reduce the heat to low.
Regularly skim off any scum that comes
to the surface. Add the sugar, shoyu
and sake, gently shaking the pan to mix
the ingredients thoroughly.

7 Cut greaseproof (waxed) paper into a
circle 1cm/½in smaller than the pan lid.
Place the paper inside the pan to seal
the ingredients. Cover with the lid and
simmer for 30 minutes, or until the sauce
has reduced by at least a half. Add the
green beans for 2 minutes so that they
just warm through.

8 Remove the paper and add the mirin.
Taste the sauce and adjust with shoyu if
required. Remove from the heat.

9 Arrange the ingredients attractively
in groups on a large serving plate.
Pour over a little sauce, and serve warm
or cold.

GRILLED VEGETABLE STICKS

FOR THIS TASTY KEBAB-STYLE DISH, MADE WITH TOFU, KONNYAKU AND AUBERGINE, YOU WILL NEED 40 BAMBOO SKEWERS, SOAKED IN WATER OVERNIGHT TO PREVENT THEM BURNING WHEN GRILLED.

SERVES FOUR

INGREDIENTS
1 × 285g/10¼oz packet tofu block
1 × 250g/9oz packet konnyaku
2 small aubergines (eggplant)
25ml/1½ tbsp toasted sesame oil
For the yellow and green sauces
45ml/3 tbsp shiro miso
15ml/1 tbsp caster (superfine) sugar
5 young spinach leaves
2.5ml/½ tsp sansho
salt
For the red sauce
15ml/1 tbsp aka miso
5ml/1 tsp caster (superfine) sugar
5ml/1 tsp mirin
To garnish
pinch of white poppy seeds
15ml/1 tbsp toasted sesame seeds

1 Drain the liquid from the tofu packet and wrap the tofu in three layers of kitchen paper. Set a chopping board on top to press out the remaining liquid. Leave for 30 minutes until the excess liquid has been absorbed by the kitchen paper. Cut into eight 7.5 × 2 × 1cm/ 3 × ¾ × ½in slices.

2 Drain the liquid from the konnyaku. Cut it in half and put in a small pan with enough water to cover. Bring to the boil and cook for about 5 minutes. Drain and cut it into eight 6 × 2 × 1cm/ 2½ × ¾ × ½in slices.

3 Cut the aubergines into two lengthways, then halve the thickness to make four flat slices. Soak in cold water for 15 minutes. Drain and pat dry.

4 To make the yellow sauce, mix the shiro miso and sugar in a pan, then cook over a low heat, stirring to dissolve the sugar. Remove from the heat. Place half the sauce in a small bowl.

5 Blanch the spinach leaves in rapidly boiling water with a pinch of salt for 30 seconds and drain, then cool under running water. Squeeze out the water and chop finely.

6 Transfer to a mortar and pound to a paste using a pestle. Mix the paste and sansho pepper into the bowl of yellow sauce to make the green sauce.

7 Put all the red sauce ingredients in a small pan and cook over a low heat, stirring constantly, until the sugar has dissolved. Remove from the heat.

8 Pierce the slices of tofu, konnyaku and aubergine with two bamboo skewers each. Heat the grill (broiler) to high. Brush the aubergine slices with sesame oil and grill (broil) for 7–8 minutes each side. Turn several times.

9 Grill the konnyaku and tofu slices for 3–5 minutes each side, or until lightly browned. Remove them from the heat but keep the grill hot.

10 Spread the red miso sauce on the aubergine slices. Spread one side of the tofu slices with green sauce and one side of the konnyaku with the yellow miso sauce from the pan. Grill the slices for 1–2 minutes. Sprinkle the aubergines with poppy seeds. Sprinkle the konnyaku with sesame seeds and serve all together.

ROLLED OMELETTE

EASIER TO MAKE THAN IT LOOKS, ALL THAT IS NEEDED TO MAKE THIS LIGHT AND SWEET OMELETTE IS A SUSHI ROLLING MAT, WRAPPED IN CLEAR FILM. USE A ROUND OR RECTANGULAR FRYING PAN.

4 Keeping the rolled omelette in the pan, push back to the farthest side from you. Oil the empty part of the pan again. Pour one-third of the egg mixture in at the empty side. Lift up the first roll with chopsticks, and let the egg mixture run underneath. When it looks half set, roll the omelette around the first roll to make a single roll with many layers.

SERVES FOUR

INGREDIENTS

  45ml/3 tbsp second dashi stock, or
    the same amount of water and a
    pinch of dashi-no-moto
  30ml/2 tbsp mirin
  15ml/1 tbsp caster (superfine) sugar
  5ml/1 tsp shoyu
  5ml/1 tsp salt
  6 large (US extra large) eggs, beaten
  vegetable oil
For the garnish
  2.5cm/1in daikon
  4 shiso leaves (optional)
  shoyu

1 Warm the dashi stock in a small pan. Mix in the mirin, sugar, shoyu and salt. Add to the beaten eggs and stir well.

2 Heat an omelette pan or a rectangular Japanese pan over a medium heat. Soak kitchen paper in a little oil and wipe the pan to grease it.

3 Pour in a quarter of the egg mixture. Tilt the pan to coat it evenly. When the omelette starts to set, roll it up towards you with chopsticks or a spatula.

5 Move the roll gently on to a sushi rolling mat covered with clear film (plastic wrap). Roll the omelette firmly into the roller mat. Leave to stand rolled up for 5 minutes. Repeat the whole process again to make another roll.

6 Grate the daikon with a daikon grater or a very fine grater. Alternatively, use a food processor. Squeeze out the juice with your hand.

7 Cut the rolled omelettes into 2.5cm/ 1in slices crossways.

8 Lay the shiso leaves, if using, on four small plates and place a few slices of the omelette on top. Put a small heap of grated daikon to one side and add a few drops of shoyu to the top.

SAVOURY EGG SOUP

THIS DELICIOUS CUSTARD-LIKE SOUP IS SOFTER AND RUNNIER THAN A WESTERN CUSTARD PUDDING.
IT CONTAINS TASTY SURPRISES, SUCH AS PINK PRAWNS AND JADE-GREEN GINGKO NUTS.

SERVES FOUR

INGREDIENTS

8 gingko nuts in shells (or canned)
4 medium raw tiger prawns (jumbo
  shrimp), peeled, heads and
  tails removed
5cm/2in carrot, thinly sliced
4 mitsuba sprigs or 8 chives
75g/3oz chicken breast portion, skinned
5ml/1 tsp sake
5ml/1 tsp shoyu
2 fresh shiitake mushrooms, thinly
  sliced, stalks discarded
salt

For the custard

3 large (US extra large) eggs, beaten
500ml/17fl oz/2⅓ cups first dashi
  stock, or the same amount of water
  and 2.5ml/½ tsp dashi-no-moto
15ml/1 tbsp sake
15ml/1 tbsp shoyu
2.5ml/½ tsp salt

1 Carefully crack the gingko nut shells with a nutcracker and boil the nuts for 5 minutes. Drain. Remove any skin.

2 Insert a cocktail stick (toothpick) into the back of each prawn and remove the vein. Blanch the prawns in hot water until they curl up. Drain and pat dry.

3 Cut the carrot slices into maple-leaf shapes with a sharp knife or a vegetable cutter. Blanch in salted water. Drain.

4 Cut off the mitsuba roots. Cut the stems 2.5cm/1in from the top and keep the leaves. Chop the stems in half and pour hot water over to wilt them. If using chives, chop into 7.5cm/3in lengths and wilt as the mitsuba stems. Put two mitsuba stems or two chives together and tie a knot in the middle.

5 Dice the chicken, then marinate in the sake and shoyu for 15 minutes.

6 To make the custard, put all the ingredients together in a bowl. Mix with chopsticks, and strain into a bowl.

7 Bring a steamer to the boil, then set the heat to very low.

8 Divide the chicken, shiitake, gingko nuts, prawns and carrots among four ramekins. Divide the egg mixture among the ramekins.

9 Put the mitsuba stems or chives on top, and the leaves if you like, and then cover each ramekin with a piece of foil. Carefully place them in the steamer. Steam on low for 15 minutes. Insert a cocktail stick into the egg: if the liquid stays clear, it's set. Serve hot.

VARIATIONS

• For a fish and shellfish variation, use scallops, crab meat, filleted lemon sole and asparagus tips.
• For a vegetarian version, try par-boiled turnips, oyster mushrooms, wakame seaweed and thinly sliced strips of spring onions (scallions).

FISH AND SHELLFISH

There are numerous delicious and healthy fish dishes in the

Japanese culinary tradition, including many using fish that is

so fresh it does not require cooking. Others employ a wide

variety of cooking methods, ranging from "cooking" the fresh

fish in vinegar, to flavouring it with seaweed, or lightly

deep-frying in tempura.

SASHIMI MORIAWASE

THE ARRANGEMENT OF A DISH OF SASHIMI IS AS IMPORTANT AS THE FRESHNESS OF THE FISH. CHOOSE TWO TO FIVE KINDS OF FISH FROM EACH GROUP AND ONLY USE THE FRESHEST CATCH OF THE DAY.

SERVES FOUR

INGREDIENTS
  500g/1¼lb total of fish from the
    4 groups
Group A, skinned fillets (cut lengthways
if possible)
  Maguro akami: lean tuna
  Maguro toro: fatty tuna
  Sake: salmon
  Kajiki: swordfish
  Tai: sea bream or red snapper
  Suzuki: sea bass
  Hamachi: yellowtail
  Katsuo: skipjack tuna
Group B, skinned fillets
  Hirame: flounder or sole
  Karei: halibut or turbot
Group C
  Ika: squid body, cleaned, boned
    and skinned
  Tako: cooked octopus tentacles
  Hotate-gai: scallop (the coral, black
    stomach and frill removed)
Group D
  Aka-ebi: sweet prawns (shrimp),
    peeled, heads can be removed,
    tails intact
  Uni: sea urchin
  Ikura: salted salmon roe
To serve
  1 fresh daikon, peeled and cut into
    6cm/2½in lengths
  1 Japanese or salad cucumber
  4 shiso leaves
  2 limes, halved (optional)
  45ml/3 tbsp wasabi paste from a
    tube, or the same amount of wasabi
    powder mixed with 20ml/4 tsp water
  1 bottle tamari shoyu

1 Make the *tsuma* (the daikon strands). Slice the daikon pieces very thinly lengthways, then cut the slices into very thin strips lengthways. Rinse thoroughly under running water, drain and put in the refrigerator.

2 Prepare the cucumber. Trim and cut into 3cm/1¼in lengths, then cut each cucumber cylinder in half lengthways.

3 Place the cucumber on a chopping board, flat-side down. Make very fine cuts across each piece, leaving the slices joined together at one side. Then, gently squeeze the cucumber together between your fingers so that the slices fan out sideways. Set them aside and cover with clear film (plastic wrap).

4 Slice the fish. Group A needs *hira giri*, a thick cut: trim the fillet into a long rectangular shape. Skin-side up, cut into 1cm/½in thick slices with the grain.

5 Group B needs *usu zukuri*, very thin slices. Place the fillet horizontally to you on its skinned side. Hold the knife almost horizontally to the fillet, shave it very thinly across the grain.

6 Group C fish each require different cutting styles. Slice the cooked octopus diagonally into 5mm/¼in thick ovals. Slice the scallops in half horizontally. If they are thicker than 4cm/1½in, slice into three.

7 Cut open the squid body and turn to lie on its skinned side, horizontally to you. Score lines 5mm/¼in apart over the surface, then cut into 5mm/¼in strips. Group D is all ready to arrange.

8 Arrange the *sashimi* creatively. First, take a handful of daikon and heap up on to the serving plate a large mound or several small mounds. Then, base your design on the following basic rules:
Group A and C Put each slice of fish side by side like domino pieces. You can lay them on a shiso leaf.
Group B Use the thin, soft slices to make a rose shape, or overlap the slices slightly, so that the texture of the plate can be seen through them.
Group D Place the prawns by their tails, 2–3 at a time, in a bundle. If the sea urchins come tightly packed in a little box, try to get them out in one piece. The salmon roe can be heaped on thin cucumber slices or scooped into a lime case, made from a half lime, flesh removed. Fill the case with some daikon and place the roe on top.

9 Arrange the cucumber fans, heaped wasabi paste and shiso leaves to perfect your design. Serve immediately. Pour some shoyu into four dishes and mix in the wasabi. As the sauce is quite salty, only dip the edge of the *sashimi* into it.

LEMON SOLE AND FRESH OYSTER SALAD

OYSTERS, FLAVOURED WITH A RICE-VINEGAR DRESSING, TASTE WONDERFUL WITH LEMON SOLE SASHIMI. IN JAPAN, MENUS ARE BASED ON WHAT FISH WAS FRESHLY CAUGHT THAT DAY, NOT THE OTHER WAY AROUND. THIS DISH IS CALLED HIRAME KONBU JIME TO NAMA-GAKI NO SALADA.

SERVES FOUR

INGREDIENTS
 1 very fresh lemon sole, skinned and
  filleted into 4 pieces
 105ml/7 tbsp rice vinegar
 dashi-konbu, in 4 pieces, big enough
  to cover the fillets
 50g/2oz Japanese cucumber, ends
  trimmed, or ordinary salad
  cucumber with seeds removed
 50g/2oz celery sticks, strings removed
 450g/1lb large broad (fava)
  beans, podded
 1 lime, ½ thinly sliced
 60ml/4 tbsp walnut oil
 seeds from ½ pomegranate
 salt
For the oysters
 15ml/1 tbsp rice vinegar
 30ml/2 tbsp shoyu
 15ml/1 tbsp sake
 12 large fresh oysters, opened
 25g/1oz daikon or radishes, peeled
  and very finely grated
 8 chives

1 Sprinkle salt on the sole fillets. Cover and cool in the refrigerator for an hour.

2 Mix the rice vinegar and a similar amount of water in a bowl. Wash the fish fillets in the mixture, then drain well. Cut each fillet in half lengthways.

3 Lay 1 piece of dashi-konbu on a work surface. Place a pair of sole fillets, skinned-sides together, on to it, then lay another piece of konbu on top. Cover all the fillets like this and chill for 3 hours.

4 Halve the cucumber crossways and slice thinly lengthways. Then slice again diagonally into 2cm/¾in wide pieces. Do the same for the celery. Sprinkle the cucumber with salt and leave to soften for 30–60 minutes. Gently squeeze to remove the moisture. Rinse if it tastes too salty, but drain well.

5 Boil the broad beans in lightly salted water for 15 minutes, or until soft. Drain and cool under running water, then peel off the skins. Sprinkle with salt.

6 Mix the rice vinegar, shoyu and sake for the oysters in a small bowl.

7 Slice the sole very thinly with a sharp knife. Remove the slightly chewy dashi-konbu first, if you prefer.

8 Place some pieces of cucumber and celery in a small mound in the centre of four serving plates, then lay lime slices on top. Garnish with some chopped chives. Place the oysters to one side of the cucumber, topped with a few broad beans, then season with 5ml/1 tsp of the vinegar mix and 10ml/2 tsp grated daikon or radishes. Arrange the sole *sashimi* on the other side and drizzle walnut oil and a little lime juice on top. Add pomegranate seeds and serve.

MARINATED SALMON WITH AVOCADO

USE ONLY THE FRESHEST OF SALMON FOR THIS DELICIOUS SALAD. THE MARINADE OF LEMON AND DASHI-KONBU "COOKS" THE SALMON, WHICH IS THEN SERVED WITH AVOCADO, TOASTED ALMONDS AND SALAD LEAVES AND ACCOMPANIED BY A MISO MAYONNAISE.

SERVES FOUR

INGREDIENTS
    250g/9oz very fresh salmon tail,
        skinned and filleted
    juice of 1 lemon
    10cm/4in dashi-konbu, wiped with a
        damp cloth and cut into 4 strips
    1 ripe avocado
    4 shiso leaves, stalks removed and
        cut in half lengthways
    about 115g/4oz mixed leaves
        such as lamb's lettuce, frisée or
        rocket (arugula)
    45ml/3 tbsp flaked (sliced) almonds,
        toasted in a dry frying pan until just
        slightly browned
For the miso mayonnaise
    90ml/6 tbsp good-quality mayonnaise
    15ml/1 tbsp shiro miso
    ground black pepper

1 Cut the first salmon fillet in half crossways at the tail end where the fillet is not wider than 4cm/1½in. Next, cut the wider part in half lengthways. This means the fillet from one side is cut into three. Cut the other fillet into three pieces, in the same way.

2 Pour the lemon juice and two of the dashi-konbu pieces into a wide shallow plastic container. Lay the salmon fillets in the base and sprinkle with the rest of the dashi-konbu. Marinate for about 15 minutes, then turn once and leave for a further 15 minutes. The salmon should change to a pink "cooked" colour. Remove the salmon from the marinade and wipe with kitchen paper.

3 Holding a very sharp knife at an angle, cut the salmon into 5mm/¼in thick slices against the grain.

4 Halve the avocado and sprinkle with a little of the remaining salmon marinade. Remove the avocado stone (pit) and skin, then carefully slice to the same thickness as the salmon.

5 Mix the miso mayonnaise ingredients in a small bowl. Spread about 5ml/1 tsp on to the back of each of the shiso leaves, then mix the remainder with 15ml/1 tbsp of the remaining marinade to loosen the mayonnaise.

6 Arrange the salad on four plates. Top with the avocado, salmon, shiso leaves and almonds, and drizzle over the remaining miso mayonnaise.

7 Alternatively, you can build a tower of avocado and salmon slices. For each serving, take an eighth of the avocado slices and place them in the centre of a plate, slightly overlapping. Add a shiso leaf, miso-side down. Then place the same number of salmon slices on top, again slightly overlapping. Repeat the process. Arrange the salad leaves and almonds, and spoon over the miso mayonnaise. Serve immediately.

SEAFOOD SALAD WITH FRUITY DRESSING

WHITE FISH IS BRIEFLY SEARED, THEN SERVED WITH PRAWNS AND SALAD TOSSED IN AN OIL-FREE APRICOT AND APPLE DRESSING. THE FRUIT FLAVOURS MAKE A DELICATE ACCOMPANIMENT TO THE FISH.

SERVES FOUR

INGREDIENTS
  1 baby onion, sliced lengthways
  lemon juice
  400g/14oz very fresh sea bream or
    sea bass, filleted
  30ml/2 tbsp sake
  4 large king prawns (jumbo shrimp),
    heads and shells removed
  about 400g/14oz mixed salad leaves
For the fruity dressing
  2 ripe apricots, skinned and
    stoned (pitted)
  ¼ apple, peeled and cored
  60ml/4 tbsp second dashi stock or
    the same amount of water and
    5ml/1 tsp dashi-no-moto
  10ml/2 tsp shoyu
  salt and ground white pepper

1 Soak the onion slices in ice-cold water for 30 minutes. Drain well.

2 Bring a pan half-full of water to the boil. Add a dash of lemon juice and plunge the fish fillet into it. Remove after 30 seconds, and cool immediately under cold running water for 30 seconds to stop the cooking. Cut into 8mm/⅓in thick slices crossways.

3 Pour the sake into a small pan, bring to the boil, then add the prawns. Cook for 1 minute, or until their colour has completely changed to pink.

4 Cool immediately under cold running water for 30 seconds to again stop the cooking. Cut the prawns into 1cm/½in thick slices crossways.

5 Slice one apricot very thinly, then set aside. Purée the remaining dressing ingredients in a food processor. Add salt, if required, and pepper. Chill.

6 Lay a small amount of mixed leaves on four plates. Mix the fish, prawn, apricot and onion slices in a bowl. Add the remaining leaves, then pour on the dressing and toss well. Heap up on the plates and serve immediately.

COOK'S TIP
You can use a knife and fork to eat these salads, of course; however, marinated fish definitely tastes better with wooden rather than metal cutlery.

TURBOT SASHIMI SALAD WITH WASABI

EATING SASHIMI, OR RAW FISH, WITH TRADITIONAL SAUCES DISAPPEARED WHEN SHOYU BECAME POPULAR IN THE 17TH CENTURY. THE USE OF SAUCES RETURNED WITH THE WESTERN-INSPIRED SALAD.

SERVES FOUR

INGREDIENTS
  ice cubes
  400g/14oz very fresh thick turbot,
    skinned and filleted
  300g/11oz mixed salad leaves
  8 radishes, thinly sliced
For the wasabi dressing
  25g/1oz rocket (arugula) leaves
  50g/2oz cucumber, chopped
  90ml/6 tbsp rice vinegar (use brown
    if available)
  75ml/5 tbsp olive oil
  5ml/1 tsp salt
  15ml/1 tbsp wasabi paste from a
    tube, or the same amount of
    wasabi powder mixed with 7.5ml/
    1½ tsp water

1 First make the dressing. Roughly tear the rocket leaves and process with the cucumber and rice vinegar in a food processor or blender. Pour into a small bowl and add the rest of the dressing ingredients, except for the wasabi. Check the seasoning and add more salt, if required. Chill until needed.

2 Chill the serving plates while you prepare the fish, if you like.

3 Prepare a bowl of cold water with a few ice cubes. Cut the turbot fillet in half lengthways, then cut into 5mm/¼in thick slices crossways. Plunge these into the ice-cold water as you slice. After 2 minutes or so, they will start to curl and become firm. Take out and drain on kitchen paper.

4 In a large bowl, mix the fish, salad leaves and radishes. Mix the wasabi into the dressing and toss well with the salad. Serve immediately.

CUBED AND MARINATED RAW TUNA

THIS DISH IS CALLED MAGURO BUTSU. *WHEN PREPARING BIG FISH LIKE TUNA OR SWORDFISH FOR SASHIMI,* JAPANESE FISHMONGERS CUT THEM LENGTHWAYS TO MAKE A LONG RECTANGULAR SHAPE. AFTER THE PRIME PARTS ARE CUT OUT, THE TRIMMINGS ARE SOLD CHEAPLY. BUTSU IS A CHOPPED TRIMMING, AND IT HAS ALL THE QUALITY OF THE BEST TUNA SASHIMI.*

SERVES FOUR

INGREDIENTS
   400g/14oz very fresh tuna, skinned
   1 carton mustard and cress (optional)
   20ml/4 tsp wasabi paste from a tube,
      or the same amount of wasabi
      powder mixed with 10ml/2 tsp water
   60ml/4 tbsp shoyu
   8 spring onions (scallions), green
      part only, finely chopped
   4 shiso leaves, cut into thin
      slivers lengthways

1 Cut the tuna into 2cm/¾in cubes. If using mustard and cress, tie into pretty bunches or arrange as a bed in four small serving bowls or plates.

2 Just 5–10 minutes before serving, blend the wasabi paste with the shoyu in a bowl, then add the tuna and spring onions. Mix well and leave to marinate for 5 minutes. Divide among the bowls and add a few slivers of shiso leaves on top. Serve immediately.

SPICY FRIED MACKEREL

THIS DISH GOES DOWN VERY WELL WITH CHILLED JAPANESE LAGER BEER. CALLED SABA TATSUTA AGGE, IT IS ALSO EXCELLENT COLD AND IS VERY GOOD SERVED WITH SALAD.

SERVES FOUR

INGREDIENTS

    675g/1½lb mackerel, filleted
    60ml/4 tbsp shoyu
    60ml/4 tbsp sake
    60ml/4 tbsp caster (superfine) sugar
    1 garlic clove, crushed
    2cm/¾in piece fresh root ginger,
      peeled and finely grated
    2–3 shiso leaves, chopped into thin
      strips (optional)
    cornflour (cornstarch), for dusting
    vegetable oil, for deep-frying
    1 lime, cut into thick wedges

VARIATION
Shiso leaves are only sold in Japanese food stores. If you can't find them, use 5–6 chopped basil leaves instead.

1 Using a pair of tweezers, remove any remaining bones from the mackerel. Cut the fillets in half lengthways, then slice diagonally crossways into bitesize pieces.

2 Mix the shoyu, sake, sugar, garlic, grated ginger and shiso in a mixing bowl to make the marinade. Add the mackerel pieces and leave to marinate for 20 minutes.

3 Drain and pat gently with kitchen paper. Dust the fillets with cornflour.

4 Heat plenty of oil in a wok or a deep-fryer. The temperature must be kept around 180°C/350°F. Deep-fry the fillets, a few pieces at a time, until the pieces turn a shiny brown colour. Drain on kitchen paper. Serve at once with wedges of lime.

SCALLOPS SASHIMI IN MUSTARD SAUCE

THE JAPANESE NAME, HOTATE KOBACHI, MEANS "SCALLOP IN A LITTLE DEEP BOWL". THIS IS A TYPICAL SERVING SIZE FOR LOTS OF JAPANESE DISHES AS A MEAL USUALLY CONSISTS OF AT LEAST THREE DISHES. IN TRADITIONAL FORMAL DINING, KAISEKI, MORE THAN A DOZEN SMALL DISHES ARE SERVED ONE AFTER ANOTHER AND THIS ELEGANT DISH CAN BE ONE OF THEM.

2 Put the dried chrysanthemum or the flower petals in a sieve. Pour hot water from a kettle all over, and leave to drain for a while. When cool, gently squeeze the excess water out. Set aside and repeat with the watercress.

3 Mix together all the ingredients for the dressing in a bowl. Add the scallops 5 minutes before serving and mix well without breaking them. Add the flower petals and watercress, then transfer to four small bowls. Serve cold. Add a little more shoyu, if required.

COOK'S TIPS

• Any white fish *sashimi* can be used in this dish.

• Substitute the watercress with the finely chopped green part of spring onions (scallions).

• Do not use chrysanthemums picked from your garden, as the edible species are different to ornamental ones. Fresh edible chrysanthemums and other edible flowers are now increasingly available at specialist Japanese stores, or look for dried ones in Asian stores.

SERVES FOUR

INGREDIENTS

    8 scallops or 16 queen scallops, cleaned and coral removed

    ¼ dried sheet chrysanthemum petals (sold as kiku nori) or a handful of edible flower petals such as yellow nasturtium

    4 bunches of watercress, leaves only

For the dressing

    30ml/2 tbsp shoyu

    5ml/1 tsp sake

    10ml/2 tsp English (hot) mustard

1 Slice the scallops in three horizontally then cut in half crossways. If you use queen scallops, slice in two horizontally.

DEEP-FRIED <u>AND</u> MARINATED SMALL FISH

THE INFLUENCE OF EARLY EUROPEANS, OR NANBAN, WHO FIRST BROUGHT DEEP-FRYING TO JAPAN A FEW HUNDRED YEARS AGO, IS STILL EVIDENT IN THIS DISH, KNOWN AS KOZAKANA NANBAN-ZUKE.

SERVES FOUR

INGREDIENTS
450g/1lb sprats (US small whitebait)
plain (all-purpose) flour, for dusting
1 small carrot
⅓ cucumber
2 spring onions (scallions)
4cm/1½in piece fresh root
  ginger, peeled
1 dried red chilli
75ml/5 tbsp rice vinegar
60ml/4 tbsp shoyu
15ml/1 tbsp mirin
30ml/2 tbsp sake
vegetable oil, for deep-frying

1 Wipe the sprats dry with kitchen paper, then put them in a small plastic bag with a handful of flour. Seal and shake vigorously to coat the fish.

2 Cut the carrot and cucumber into thin strips by hand or using a mandolin or food processor. Cut the spring onions into three, then slice into thin, lengthways strips. Slice the ginger into thin, lengthways strips and rinse in cold water. Drain. Seed and chop the chilli into thin rings.

VARIATION
You can use small sardines, too. They have tougher bones and need to be deep-fried twice. Heat the oil and deep-fry until the outside of the fish is just crisp but still pale. Drain on kitchen paper and wait for 5 minutes. This process cooks the fish through before the coating starts to burn. Put them back into the oil again until deep golden brown.

3 In a mixing bowl, mix the rice vinegar, shoyu, mirin and sake together to make a marinade. Add the chilli and all the sliced vegetables. Stir well using a pair of chopsticks.

4 Pour plenty of oil into a deep pan and heat to 180°C/350°F. Deep-fry the fish five or six at a time until golden brown. Drain on layered kitchen paper, then plunge the hot fish into the marinade. Leave to marinate for at least an hour, stirring occasionally.

5 Serve the fish cold in a shallow bowl and put the marinated vegetables on top. This dish will keep for about a week in the refrigerator.

COOK'S TIP
The tiny sprats (US small whitebait) used here are eaten whole.

SIMMERED SQUID AND DAIKON

IKA TO DAIKON NI IS A CLASSIC DISH, THE SECRET OF WHICH USED TO BE HANDED DOWN FROM MOTHER TO DAUGHTER. NOWADAYS, YOU ARE MORE LIKELY TO TASTE THE REAL THING AT RESTAURANTS, BUT SOME GRANDMOTHERS STILL CELEBRATE FAMILY REUNIONS BY COOKING THIS HEARTY DISH.

SERVES FOUR

INGREDIENTS
   450g/1lb squid, cleaned, body and
      tentacles separated
   about 1kg/2¼lb daikon, peeled
   900ml/1½ pints/3¾ cups second
      dashi stock or the same amount of
      water and 5ml/1 tsp dashi-no-moto
   60ml/4 tbsp shoyu
   45ml/3 tbsp sake
   15ml/1 tbsp caster (superfine) sugar
   30ml/2 tbsp mirin
   grated rind of ½ yuzu or lime,
      to garnish

COOK'S TIP
When buying daikon look for one that is at least 7.5cm/3in in diameter, with a shiny, undamaged skin, and that sounds dense and heavy when you pat it.

1 Separate the two triangular flaps from the squid body. Cut the body into 1cm/½in thick rings. Cut the triangular flaps into 1cm/½in strips. Cut off and discard 2.5cm/1in from the thin end of the tentacles. Chop the tentacles into 4cm/1½in lengths.

2 Cut the daikon into 3cm/1¼in thick rounds and shave the edges of the sections with a sharp knife. Plunge the slices into cold water. Drain just before cooking.

3 Put the daikon and squid in a heavy pan and pour on the stock. Bring to the boil, and cook for 5 minutes, skimming constantly. Reduce the heat to low and add the shoyu, sake, sugar and mirin. Cover the surface with a circle of greaseproof (waxed) paper cut 2.5cm/1in smaller than the lid of the pan, and simmer for 45 minutes, shaking the pan occasionally. The liquid will reduce by almost a half.

4 Leave to stand for 5 minutes and serve hot in small bowls with a sprinkle of yuzu or lime rind.

SALMON TERIYAKI

SAKÉ TERIYAKI IS A WELL-KNOWN JAPANESE DISH, WHICH USES A SWEET AND SHINY SAUCE FOR MARINATING AS WELL AS FOR GLAZING THE INGREDIENTS.

SERVES FOUR

INGREDIENTS
   4 small salmon fillets with skin on,
      each weighing about 150g/5oz
   50g/2oz/¼ cup beansprouts, washed
   50g/2oz mangetouts (snow peas),
      ends trimmed
   20g/¾oz carrot, cut into thin strips
   salt
For the *teriyaki* sauce
   45ml/3 tbsp shoyu
   45ml/3 tbsp sake
   45ml/3 tbsp mirin
   15ml/1 tbsp plus 10ml/2 tsp caster
      (superfine) sugar

1 Mix all the ingredients for the *teriyaki* sauce except for the 10ml/2 tsp sugar, in a pan. Heat to dissolve the sugar. Remove and cool for an hour.

2 Place the salmon fillet in a shallow glass or china dish and pour over the *teriyaki* sauce. Leave to marinate for 30 minutes.

3 Meanwhile, boil the vegetables in lightly salted water. First add the beansprouts, then after 1 minute, the mangetouts. Leave for 1 minute again, and then add the thin carrot strips. Remove the pan from the heat after 1 minute, then drain the vegetables and keep warm.

4 Preheat the grill (broiler) to medium. Take the salmon fillet out of the sauce and pat dry with kitchen paper. Reserve the sauce. Lightly oil a grilling (broiling) tray. Grill (broil) the salmon for about 6 minutes, carefully turning once, until golden on both sides.

5 Pour the sauce into the pan. Add the remaining sugar and heat until dissolved. Remove from the heat. Brush the salmon with the sauce, then grill until the surface of the fish bubbles. Turn over and repeat on the other side.

6 Heap the vegetables on to serving plates. Place the salmon on top and spoon over the rest of the sauce.

CRAB MEAT IN VINEGAR

A REFRESHING SUMMER TSUMAMI (A DISH THAT ACCOMPANIES ALCOHOLIC DRINKS). FOR THE DRESSING, USE A JAPANESE OR GREEK CUCUMBER, IF POSSIBLE – THEY ARE ABOUT ONE-THIRD OF THE SIZE OF ORDINARY SALAD CUCUMBERS AND CONTAIN LESS WATER.

SERVES FOUR

INGREDIENTS
  ½ red (bell) pepper, seeded
  pinch of salt
  275g/10oz cooked white crab meat,
    or 2 × 165g/5½oz canned white
    crab meat, drained
  about 300g/11oz Japanese or
    salad cucumber
For the vinegar mixture
  15ml/1 tbsp rice vinegar
  10ml/2 tsp caster (superfine) sugar
  10ml/2 tsp awakuchi shoyu

1 Slice the red pepper into thin strips lengthways. Sprinkle with a little salt and leave for about 15 minutes. Rinse well and drain.

2 For the vinegar mixture, combine the rice vinegar, sugar and awakuchi shoyu in a small bowl.

3 Loosen the crab meat with cooking chopsticks and mix it with the sliced red pepper in a mixing bowl. Divide among four small bowls.

4 If you use salad cucumber, scoop out the seeds. Finely grate the cucumber with a fine-toothed grater or use a food processor. Drain in a fine-meshed sieve.

5 Mix the cucumber with the vinegar mixture, and pour a quarter on to the crab meat mixture in each bowl. Serve cold immediately, before the cucumber loses its colour.

VARIATIONS
• The vinegar mixture is best made using awakuchi shoyu, but ordinary shoyu can be used instead. It will make a darker dressing, however.
• This dressing can be made into a low-fat substitute for vinaigrette: reduce the sugar by half and add a few drops of oil.

ROLLED SARDINES WITH PLUM PASTE

JAPANESE COOKS SEEK TO TASTE AND EXPRESS THE SEASON IN THEIR COOKING, AND MENUS ALWAYS INCLUDE SOME SEASONAL INGREDIENTS. THIS DISH, IWASHI NO UMÉ MAKI YAKI, IS ONE OF MANY RECIPES TO CELEBRATE THE ARRIVAL OF THE HARVEST, WHEN THE SARDINE SEASON PEAKS IN AUTUMN.

SERVES FOUR

INGREDIENTS

   8 sardines, cleaned and filleted
   5ml/1 tsp salt
   4 umeboshi, about 30g/1¼oz total
    weight (choose the soft type)
   5ml/1 tsp sake
   5ml/1 tsp toasted sesame seeds
   16 shiso leaves, cut in
    half lengthways
   1 lime, thinly sliced, the centre
    hollowed out to make rings,
    to garnish

COOK'S TIP

Sardines deteriorate very quickly and must be bought and eaten on the same day. Be careful when buying: the eyes and gills should not be too pink. If the fish "melts" like cheese when grilled, don't bother to eat it.

1 Carefully cut the sardine fillets in half lengthways and place them side by side in a large, shallow container. Sprinkle with salt on both sides.

2 Remove the stones (pits) from the umeboshi and put the fruit in a small mixing bowl with the sake and toasted sesame seeds. With the back of a fork, mash the umeboshi, mixing well to form a smooth paste.

3 Wipe the sardine fillets with kitchen paper. With a butter knife, spread some umeboshi paste thinly on to one of the sardine fillets, then press some shiso leaves on top. Roll up the sardine starting from the tail and pierce with a wooden cocktail stick (toothpick). Repeat to make 16 rolled sardines.

4 Preheat the grill (broiler) to high. Lay a sheet of foil on a baking tray, and arrange the sardine rolls on this, spaced well apart to prevent sticking. Grill (broil) for 4–6 minutes on each side, or until golden brown, turning once.

5 Lay a few lime rings on four individual plates and arrange the rolled sardines alongside. Serve hot.

CLAMS AND SPRING ONIONS WITH MISO AND MUSTARD SAUCE

THE JAPANESE ARE REALLY FOND OF SHELLFISH, AND CLAMS ARE AMONG THE MOST POPULAR. IN SEASON, THEY BECOME SWEET AND JUICY, AND ARE EXCELLENT WITH THIS SWEET-AND-SOUR DRESSING.

SERVES FOUR

INGREDIENTS
   900g/2lb carpet shell clams or
     cockles, or 300g/11oz can baby
     clams in brine, or 130g/4½oz
     cooked and shelled cockles
   15ml/1 tbsp sake
   8 spring onions (scallions), green and
     white parts separated, then chopped
     in half
   10g/¼oz dried wakame
For the *nuta* dressing
   60ml/4 tbsp shiro miso
   20ml/4 tsp caster (superfine) sugar
   30ml/2 tbsp sake
   15ml/1 tbsp rice vinegar
   about 1.5ml/¼ tsp salt
   7.5ml/1½ tsp English (hot) mustard
   sprinkling of dashi-no-moto (if using
     canned shellfish)

1 If using fresh clams or cockles, wash the shells under running water. Discard any that remain open when tapped.

2 Pour 1cm/½in water into a small pan and add the clams or cockles. Sprinkle with the sake, cover, then bring to the boil. Cook over a vigorous heat for 5 minutes after the water reaches boiling point. Remove from the heat and leave to stand for 2 minutes. Discard any shells which remain closed.

3 Drain the shells and keep the liquid in a small bowl. Wait until the shells have cooled slightly, then remove the meat from most of the shells.

4 Cook the white part of the spring onions in a pan of rapidly boiling water, then add the remaining green parts after 2 minutes. Cook for 4 minutes altogether. Drain well.

5 Mix the shiro miso, sugar, sake, rice vinegar and salt for the *nuta* dressing, in a small pan. Stir in 45ml/3 tbsp of the reserved clam liquid, or the same amount of water and dashi-no-moto, if using canned shellfish.

6 Put the pan on a medium heat and stir constantly. When the sugar has dissolved, add the mustard. Check the seasoning and add a little more salt if desired. Remove from the heat and leave to cool.

7 Soak the wakame in a bowl of water for 10 minutes. Drain and squeeze out excess moisture by hand.

8 Mix together the clams or cockles, onions, wakame and dressing in a bowl. Heap up in a large bowl or divide among four small bowls and serve cold.

DEEP-FRIED SMALL PRAWNS AND CORN

THIS DISH IS CALLED KAKIAGÉ, *AN INEXPENSIVE AND INFORMAL STYLE OF TEMPURA. THIS IS ONLY ONE OF MANY VERSIONS AND IT IS A GOOD WAY OF USING UP SMALL QUANTITIES OF VEGETABLES.*

SERVES FOUR

INGREDIENTS
　200g/7oz small cooked, peeled
　　prawns (shrimp)
　4–5 button (white) mushrooms
　4 spring onions (scallions)
　75g/3oz/½ cup canned, drained or
　　frozen corn kernels, thawed
　30ml/2 tbsp frozen peas, thawed
　vegetable oil, for deep-frying
　chives, to garnish
For the tempura batter
　300ml/½ pint/1¼ cups ice-cold water
　2 eggs, beaten
　150g/5oz/1¼ cups plain
　　(all-purpose) flour
　1.5ml/¼ tsp baking powder
For the dipping sauce
　400ml/14fl oz/1⅔ cups second dashi
　　stock, or the same amount of water
　　and 5ml/1 tsp dashi-no-moto
　100ml/3fl oz/scant ½ cup shoyu
　100ml/3fl oz/scant ½ cup mirin
　15ml/1 tbsp chopped chives

1 Roughly chop half the prawns. Cut the mushrooms into small cubes. Slice the white part from the spring onions and chop this roughly.

2 To make the tempura batter, in a medium mixing bowl, mix the cold water and eggs. Add the flour and baking powder, and very roughly fold in with a pair of chopsticks or a fork. Do not beat. The batter should still be quite lumpy. Heat plenty of oil in a wok or a deep-fryer to 170°C/338°F.

3 Mix the prawns and vegetables into the batter. Pour a quarter of the batter into a small bowl, then drop gently into the oil. Using wooden spoons, carefully gather the scattered batter to form a fist-size ball. Deep-fry until golden. Drain on kitchen paper.

4 In a small pan, mix all the liquid dipping-sauce ingredients together and bring to the boil, then immediately turn off the heat. Sprinkle with chives.

5 Garnish the *kakiage* with chives, and serve with the dipping sauce.

SEAFOOD, CHICKEN AND VEGETABLE HOTPOT

THIS DISH, CALLED YOSE NABE, *IS COOKED AND EATEN AT THE TABLE, TRADITIONALLY USING A CLAY POT. YOU CAN USE A FLAMEPROOF CASSEROLE AND WILL NEED A PORTABLE TABLE-TOP STOVE.*

SERVES FOUR

INGREDIENTS
   225g/8oz salmon, scaled and cut into
     5cm/2in thick steaks with bones
   225g/8oz white fish (sea bream, cod,
     plaice or haddock), cleaned and
     scaled then chopped into 4 chunks
   300g/11oz chicken thighs, cut into
     large bitesize chunks with bones
   4 hakusai leaves, base part trimmed
   115g/4oz spinach
   1 large carrot, cut into 5mm/¼in
     thick rounds or flower shapes
   8 fresh shiitake mushrooms, stalks
     removed, or 150g/5oz oyster
     mushrooms, base trimmed
   2 thin leeks, washed and cut
     diagonally into 5cm/2in lengths
   285g/10¼oz packet tofu block,
     drained and cut into 16 cubes
   salt
For the hot-pot liquid
   12 × 6cm/4½ × 2½in dashi-konbu
   1.2 litres/2 pints/5 cups water
   120ml/4fl oz/½ cup sake
For the condiments
   90g/3½oz daikon, peeled
   1 dried chilli, halved and seeded
   1 lemon, cut into 16 wedges
   4 spring onions (scallions), chopped
   2 × 5g/⅛oz packets kezuri-bushi
   1 bottle shoyu

1 Arrange the various prepared fish and chicken on a large serving platter.

2 Boil plenty of water in a large pan and cook the hakusai for 3 minutes. Drain in a sieve and leave to cool. Add a pinch of salt to the water and boil the spinach for 1 minute, then drain in a sieve under running water.

3 Squeeze the spinach and lay on a sushi rolling mat, then roll it up firmly. Leave to rest, then unwrap and take the cylinder out. Lay the hakusai leaves next to each other on the mat. Put the cylinder in the middle and roll again firmly. Leave for 5 minutes, then unroll and cut into 5cm/2in long cylinders.

4 Transfer the hakusai cylinders to the platter along with all the remaining vegetables and the tofu.

5 Lay the dashi-konbu on the bottom of the clay pot or flameproof casserole. Mix the water and sake in a small bowl.

6 Insert a metal skewer into the cut side of the daikon two to three times, and insert the chilli pieces. Leave for about 5 minutes, then grate finely. Drain in a fine-meshed sieve and squeeze the liquid out. Shape the pink daikon into a mound and put in a bowl. Put all the other condiments into small bowls.

7 Fill the pot or casserole with two-thirds of the water and sake mixture. Bring to the boil, then reduce the heat.

8 Put the carrot, shiitake, chicken and salmon into the pot. When the colour of the meat and fish changes, add the rest of the ingredients in batches.

9 Guests pour a little soy sauce into small bowls, and squeeze in a little lemon juice, then mix with a condiment. Pick up the food with chopsticks and dip into the sauce. Cook more ingredients as you go, adding more water and sake as the stock reduces.

PAPER-WRAPPED and STEAMED RED SNAPPER

ORIGINALLY, THIS ELEGANT DISH FEATURED A WHOLE RED SNAPPER WRAPPED IN LAYERED JAPANESE HAND-MADE PAPER SOAKED IN SAKE AND TIED WITH RIBBONS. THIS VERSION IS A LITTLE EASIER.

4 At each end, fold the top corners down diagonally, then fold the bottom corners up to meet the opposite folded edge to make a triangle. Press flat with your palm. Repeat the process to make four parcels.

5 Cut 2.5cm/1in from the tip of the asparagus, and slice in half lengthways. Slice the asparagus stems and spring onions diagonally into thin ovals. Par-boil the tips for 1 minute in lightly salted water and drain. Set aside.

6 Open the parcels. Place the asparagus slices and the spring onions inside. Sprinkle with salt and place the fish on top. Add more salt and some sake, then sprinkle in the lime rind. Refold the parcels.

SERVES FOUR

INGREDIENTS
4 small red snapper fillets, no greater than 18 × 6cm/7 × 2½in, or whole snapper, 20cm/8in long, gutted but head, tail and fins intact
8 asparagus spears, hard ends discarded
4 spring onions (scallions)
60ml/4 tbsp sake
grated rind of ½ lime
½ lime, thinly sliced
5ml/1 tsp shoyu (optional)
salt

1 Sprinkle the red snapper fillets with salt on both sides and leave in the refrigerator for 20 minutes. Preheat the oven to 180°C/350°F/Gas 4.

2 To make the parcels, lay greaseproof (waxed) paper measuring 38 × 30cm/ 15 × 12in on a work surface. Use two pieces for extra thickness. Fold up one-third of the paper and turn back 1cm/½in from one end to make a flap.

3 Fold 1cm/½in in from the other end to make another flap. Fold the top edge down to fold over the first flap. Interlock the two flaps to form a long rectangle.

7 Pour hot water from a kettle into a deep roasting pan fitted with a wire rack to 1cm/½in below the rack. Place the parcels on the rack. Cook in the centre of the preheated oven for 20 minutes. Check by carefully unfolding a parcel from one triangular side. The fish should have changed from translucent to white.

8 Transfer the parcels on to individual plates. Unfold both triangular ends on the plate and lift open the middle a little. Insert a thin slice of lime and place two asparagus tips on top. Serve immediately, asking your guests to open their own parcels. Add a little shoyu, if you like.

TEMPURA SEAFOOD

THIS QUINTESSENTIALLY JAPANESE DISH ACTUALLY HAS ITS ORIGINS IN THE WEST, AS TEMPURA WAS INTRODUCED TO JAPAN BY PORTUGUESE TRADERS IN THE 17TH CENTURY.

SERVES FOUR

INGREDIENTS
    8 large raw prawns (shrimp), heads
      and shells removed, tails intact
    130g/4½oz squid body, cleaned
      and skinned
    115g/4oz whiting fillets
    4 fresh shiitake mushrooms,
      stalks removed
    8 okra
    ⅛ nori sheet, 5 × 4cm/2 × 1½in
    20g/¾oz dried harusame (a packet is
      a 150–250g/5–9oz mass)
    vegetable oil and sesame oil,
      for deep-frying
    plain (all-purpose) flour, for dusting
    salt
For the dipping sauce
    400ml/14fl oz/1⅔ cups second dashi
      stock, or the same amount of water
      mixed with 5ml/1 tsp dashi-no-moto
    200ml/7fl oz/scant 1 cup shoyu
    200ml/7fl oz/scant 1 cup mirin
For the condiment
    450g/1lb daikon, peeled
    4cm/1½in fresh root ginger, peeled
      and finely grated
For the tempura batter
    ice-cold water
    1 large (US extra large) egg, beaten
    200g/7oz/2 cups plain flour, sifted
    2–3 ice cubes

1 Remove the vein from the prawns, then make 4 × 3mm/⅛in deep cuts across the belly to stop the prawns curling up. Snip the tips of the tails and gently squeeze out any liquid. Pat dry.

2 Cut open the squid body. Lay flat, inside down, on a chopping board, and make shallow criss-cross slits on one side. Cut into 2.5 × 6cm/1 × 2½in rectangular strips. Cut the whiting fillets into similar-size strips.

3 Make two notched slits on the shiitake caps, in the form of a cross. Sprinkle your hands with some salt and rub over the okra, then wash the okra under running water to clean the surface.

4 Cut the nori into four long strips lengthways. Loosen the harusame noodles from the block and cut both ends with scissors to get a few strips. Make four bunches and tie them in the middle by wrapping with a nori strip. Wet the end to fix it.

5 Make the dipping sauce. In a pan, mix all the dipping-sauce ingredients and bring to the boil, then immediately remove from the heat. Set aside and keep warm.

6 Prepare the condiment. Grate the daikon very finely. Drain in a sieve, then squeeze out any excess water by hand. Lay clear film (plastic wrap) over an egg cup and press about 2.5ml/½ tsp grated ginger into the bottom. Add 30ml/2 tbsp grated daikon. Press and invert on to a small plate. Make three more.

7 Half-fill a pan or wok with 3 parts vegetable oil to 1 part sesame oil. Bring to 175°C/347°F over a medium heat.

8 Meanwhile, make the tempura batter. Add enough ice-cold water to the egg to make 150ml/¼ pint/⅔ cup, then pour into a large bowl. Add the flour and mix roughly with chopsticks. Do not beat; leave the batter lumpy. Add some ice cubes later to keep the temperature cool.

9 Dip the okra into the batter and deep-fry until golden. Drain on a rack. Batter the underside of the shiitake. Deep-fry.

10 Increase the heat a little, then fry the harusame by holding the nori tie with chopsticks and dipping them into the oil for a few seconds. The noodles instantly turn crisp and white. Drain on kitchen paper and sprinkle with salt.

11 Hold the tail of a prawn, dust with flour, then dip into the batter. Do not put batter on the tail. Slide the prawn into the hot oil very slowly. Deep-fry one to two prawns at a time until crisp.

12 Dust the whiting strips, dip into the batter, then deep-fry until golden. Wipe the squid strips well with kitchen paper, dust with flour, then dip in batter. Deep-fry until the batter is crisp.

13 Drain excess oil from the tempura on a wire rack for a few minutes, then arrange them on individual plates. Set the condiment alongside the tempura. Reheat the dipping sauce to warm through, then pour into four small bowls.

14 Serve. Invite your guests to mix the condiment into the dipping sauce and dunk the tempura as they eat.

MARINATED AND GRILLED SWORDFISH

IN MEDIEVAL TIMES, SAIKYO (THE WESTERN CAPITAL OF ANCIENT JAPAN) HAD A VERY SOPHISTICATED CULTURE. ARISTOCRATS COMPETED WITH EACH OTHER AS TO THEIR CHEF'S SKILLS, AND MANY OF THE CLASSIC RECIPES OF TODAY ARE FROM THIS PERIOD. KAJIKI SAIKYO YAKI IS ONE SUCH EXAMPLE.

SERVES FOUR

INGREDIENTS
    4 × 175g/6oz swordfish steaks
    2.5ml/½ tsp salt
    300g/11oz saikyo or shiro miso
    45ml/3 tbsp sake
For the asparagus
    25ml/1½ tbsp shoyu
    25ml/1½ tbsp sake
    8 asparagus spears, the hard ends
      discarded, each spear cut
      into three

1 Place the swordfish in a shallow container. Sprinkle with the salt on both sides and leave for 2 hours. Drain and wipe the fish with kitchen paper.

2 Mix the miso and sake, then spread half across the bottom of the cleaned container. Cover with a sheet of muslin (cheesecloth) the size of a dishtowel, folded in half, then open the fold. Place the swordfish, side by side, on top, and cover with the muslin. Spread the rest of the miso mixture on the muslin. Make sure the muslin is touching the fish. Marinate for 2 days in the coolest part of the refrigerator.

3 Preheat the grill (broiler) to medium. Oil the wire rack and grill (broil) the fish slowly for about 8 minutes on each side, turning every 2 minutes. If the steaks are thin, check every time you turn the fish to see if they are ready.

4 Mix the shoyu and sake in a bowl. Grill the asparagus for 2 minutes on each side, then dip into the bowl. Return to the grill for 2 minutes more on each side. Dip into the sauce again and set aside.

5 Serve the steak hot on four individual serving plates. Garnish with the drained, grilled asparagus.

TEPPAN TAKI

MANY JAPANESE HOMES HAVE A PORTABLE GAS STOVE, A TABLE GRIDDLE (TEPPAN), OR A TABLE EQUIPPED WITH A RECESSED COOKING SURFACE. THIS IS BECAUSE THE JAPANESE LOVE COOKING AS THEY EAT, AND EATING AS THEY COOK. IT'S FUN TO TRY.

SERVES FOUR

INGREDIENTS
275g/10oz monkfish tail
4 large scallops, cleaned and
  corals separated
250g/9oz squid body, cleaned
  and skinned
12 raw king or tiger prawns (jumbo
  shrimp), shells and heads removed,
  tails intact
115g/4oz/½ cup beansprouts, washed
1 red (bell) pepper, seeded and cut
  into 2.5cm/1in wide strips
8 fresh shiitake mushrooms,
  stalks removed
1 red onion, cut into 5mm/¼in
  thick rounds
1 courgette (zucchini), cut into
  1cm/½in thick rounds
3 garlic cloves, thinly sliced
  lengthways
vegetable oil, for frying
Sauce A, radish and chilli sauce
8 radishes, finely grated
1 dried chilli, seeded and crushed
15ml/1 tbsp toasted sesame oil
½ onion, finely chopped
90ml/6 tbsp shoyu
30ml/2 tbsp caster (superfine) sugar
45ml/3 tbsp toasted sesame seeds
juice of ½ orange or 30ml/2 tbsp
  unsweetened orange juice
Sauce B, wasabi mayonnaise
105ml/7 tbsp mayonnaise
15ml/1 tbsp wasabi paste from a
  tube, or the same amount of
  wasabi powder mixed with 15ml/
  1 tbsp water
5ml/1 tsp shoyu
Sauce C, lime and soy sauce
juice of 1 lime
grated rind of 1 lime
20ml/4 tsp sake
90ml/6 tbsp shoyu
1 bunch chives, finely chopped

1 Sauce A Mix the grated radish with its juice and the chilli in a bowl. Heat the sesame oil in a frying pan and fry the onion until soft.

2 Pour in the shoyu and add the sugar and sesame seeds, removing the pan from the heat just as it starts to boil. Tip into the bowl and add the orange juice. Stir well and leave to cool.

3 Sauce B and C Mix the ingredients separately in small bowls, cover with clear film (plastic wrap) and set aside.

4 Cut the monkfish into large, bitesize, 5mm/¼in thick slices. Cut the scallops in half horizontally.

5 With a small sharp knife, make shallow criss-cross slits in the skinned side of the squid. Slice into 2.5 x 4cm/ 1 x 1½in pieces.

6 Place all the seafood on half of a serving platter, and arrange all the prepared vegetables (apart from the garlic) on the other half. Divide sauces A and C among eight small dishes; these are for dipping. Put the wasabi mayonnaise in a small bowl with a teaspoon. Prepare serving plates as well.

7 Heat the griddle on the table and oil it with a brush or kitchen paper. First, fry the garlic slices until crisp and golden. Remove the garlic chips to a small dish to mix with any sauces you like. Then fry the ingredients as you eat, dipping into the sauces or serving them with the wasabi mayonnaise. Oil the griddle from time to time.

POULTRY
AND MEAT

Most meat recipes in Japanese cooking use the meat as a rich

flavouring ingredient for vegetables and rice. Even in

sukiyaki, *the quintessential meat dish, plenty of vegetables*

of different textures and flavours accompany the meat.

Sauces and stocks are also used to enhance the meat's flavour.

GRILLED SKEWERED CHICKEN

THE JAPANESE ALWAYS ACCOMPANY DRINK WITH NIBBLES. THE NIBBLES ARE GENERALLY CALLED TSUMAMI, AND GRILLED SKEWERED CHICKEN DIPPED IN YAKITORI *SAUCE IS ONE OF THE MOST POPULAR. THERE ARE THOUSANDS OF DEDICATED* YAKITORI *BARS IN JAPAN.*

SERVES FOUR

INGREDIENTS
    8 chicken thighs with skin, boned
    8 large, thick spring onions
        (scallions), trimmed
For the *yakitori* sauce
    60ml/4 tbsp sake
    75ml/5 tbsp shoyu
    15ml/1 tbsp mirin
    15ml/1 tbsp caster (superfine) sugar
To serve
    shichimi togarashi, sansho or
        lemon wedges

1 First, make the *yakitori* sauce. Mix all the ingredients together in a small pan. Bring to the boil, then reduce the heat and simmer for 10 minutes, or until the sauce has thickened.

2 Cut the chicken into 2.5cm/1in cubes. Cut the spring onions into 2.5cm/1in long sticks.

3 To grill (broil), preheat the grill (broiler) to high. Oil the wire rack and spread out the chicken cubes on it. Grill both sides of the chicken until the juices drip, then dip the pieces in the sauce and put back on the rack. Grill for 30 seconds on each side, repeating the dipping process twice more.

4 Set aside and keep warm. Gently grill the spring onions until soft and slightly brown outside. Do not dip. Thread about four pieces of chicken and three spring onion pieces on to each of eight bamboo skewers.

5 Alternatively, to cook on a barbecue, soak eight bamboo skewers overnight in water. This prevents the skewers from burning. Prepare the barbecue. Thread the chicken and spring onion pieces on to skewers, as above. Place the sauce in a small bowl with a brush.

6 Cook the skewered chicken on the barbecue. Keep the skewer handles away from the fire, turning them frequently until the juices start to drip. Brush the chicken with sauce. Return to the coals and repeat this process twice more until the chicken is well cooked.

7 Arrange the skewers on a platter and serve sprinkled with shichimi togarashi or sansho, or accompanied by lemon wedges.

GRILLED CHICKEN BALLS COOKED ON BAMBOO SKEWERS

THESE TASTY CHICKEN BALLS, KNOWN AS TSUKUNE, ARE ANOTHER YAKITORI BAR REGULAR AS WELL AS A FAVOURITE FAMILY DISH, AS IT IS EASY FOR CHILDREN TO EAT DIRECTLY FROM THE SKEWER. YOU CAN MAKE THE BALLS IN ADVANCE UP TO THE END OF STEP 2, AND THEY FREEZE VERY WELL.

SERVES FOUR

INGREDIENTS
  300g/11oz skinless chicken,
    minced (ground)
  2 eggs
  2.5ml/½ tsp salt
  10ml/2 tsp plain (all-purpose) flour
  10ml/2 tsp cornflour (cornstarch)
  90ml/6 tbsp dried breadcrumbs
  2.5cm/1in piece fresh root
    ginger, grated
For the *"tare" yakitori* sauce
  60ml/4 tbsp sake
  75ml/5 tbsp shoyu
  15ml/1 tbsp mirin
  15ml/1 tbsp caster (superfine) sugar
  2.5ml/½ tsp cornflour (cornstarch)
    blended with 5ml/1 tsp water
To serve
  shichimi togarashi or
    sansho (optional)

1 Soak eight bamboo skewers overnight in water. Put all the ingredients for the chicken balls, except the ginger, in a food processor and blend well.

2 Wet your hands and scoop about a tablespoonful of the mixture into your palm. Shape it into a small ball about half the size of a golf ball. Make a further 30–32 balls in the same way.

3 Squeeze the juice from the grated ginger into a small mixing bowl. Discard the pulp.

4 Add the ginger juice to a small pan of boiling water. Add the chicken balls, and boil for about 7 minutes, or until the colour of the meat changes and the balls float to the surface. Scoop out using a slotted spoon and drain on a plate covered with kitchen paper.

5 In a small pan, mix all the ingredients for the *yakitori* sauce, except for the cornflour liquid. Bring to the boil, then reduce the heat and simmer for about 10 minutes, or until the sauce has slightly reduced. Add the cornflour liquid and stir until the sauce is thick. Transfer to a small bowl.

6 Thread 3–4 balls on to each skewer. Cook under a medium grill (broiler) or on a barbecue, keeping the skewer handles away from the fire. Turn them frequently for a few minutes, or until the balls start to brown. Brush with sauce and return to the heat. Repeat the process twice. Serve, sprinkled with shichimi togarashi or sansho, if you like.

SUKIYAKI

YOU WILL NEED A SUKIYAKI PAN OR A SHALLOW CAST-IRON PAN, AND A PORTABLE TABLE STOVE TO COOK THIS TRADITIONAL DISH OF BEEF AND VEGETABLES.

SERVES FOUR

INGREDIENTS

   600g/1lb 5oz well-marbled beef
     sirloin, without bone, sliced into
     3mm/⅛in slices
   15ml/1 tbsp sake
   1 packet shirataki noodles, about
     200g/7oz, drained
   2 large onions, cut into 8 slices
     lengthways
   450g/1lb enokitake mushrooms,
     root part removed
   12 shiitake mushrooms,
     stalks removed
   10 spring onions (scallions), trimmed
     and quartered diagonally lengthways
   300g/11oz shungiku, cut in half
     lengthways, or watercress
   250–275g/9–10oz tofu, drained and
     cut into 8–12 large bitesize cubes
   4–8 very fresh eggs, at room
     temperature
   about 20g/¾oz beef fat
For the *wari-shita* sauce
   75ml/5 tbsp second dashi stock, or
     the same amount of water and
     5ml/1 tsp dashi-no-moto
   75ml/5 tbsp shoyu
   120ml/4fl oz/½ cup mirin
   15ml/1 tbsp sake
   15ml/1 tbsp caster (superfine) sugar

1 Arrange the beef slices on a large serving plate. Sprinkle with the sake and leave to settle.

2 Par-boil the shirataki in rapidly boiling water for 2 minutes, then drain. Wash under cold running water and cut into 5cm/2in lengths. Drain well.

3 Mix all the ingredients for the *wari-shita* sauce in a small pan and place over a medium heat until the sugar has dissolved. Pour into a jug (pitcher) or bowl.

4 On a tray, arrange all the vegetables, shirataki and tofu. Break one egg into each of four small serving bowls. Take everything to the table.

5 Start cooking when the guests are seated at the table. Heat the pan on a table cooker until very hot, then reduce the heat to medium, and add some beef fat. When it has melted, add the spring onions and onion slices, then increase the heat. Stir-fry for 2 minutes, or until the onions become soft. The guests should now start to beat the egg in their bowls.

6 Add a quarter of the *wari-shita* sauce to the pan. When it starts to bubble, add about a quarter of the vegetables, tofu and shirataki. Place them side by side but do not mix them. Keep some space clear for the beef.

7 Cook one beef slice per guest at a time. Put four slices in the space you kept in the pan. As they change colour, remove them immediately from the pan and dip them into the beaten egg. Eat straight away. Cook the vegetables and other ingredients in the same way; they might take 10–15 minutes to cook. Add the remaining ingredients as you eat. Add more *wari-shita* sauce when it is reduced in the pan. Add another egg to the dipping bowls if required.

PAPER-THIN SLICED BEEF COOKED IN STOCK

THE JAPANESE NAME FOR THIS DISH, SHABU SHABU, REFERS TO "WASHING" THE WAFER-THIN SLICES OF BEEF IN HOT STOCK. YOU WILL NEED A PORTABLE STOVE TO COOK THIS MEAL AT THE TABLE.

SERVES FOUR

INGREDIENTS
600g/1lb 5oz boneless beef sirloin
2 thin leeks, trimmed and cut into
   2 × 5cm/¾ × 2in strips
4 spring onions (scallions), quartered
8 shiitake mushrooms, less stalks
175g/6oz oyster mushrooms, base
   part removed, torn into small pieces
½ hakusai, base part removed and
   cut into 5cm/2in squares
300g/11oz shungiku, halved
275g/10oz tofu, halved then cut in
   2cm/¾in thick slices crossways
10 × 6cm/4 × 2½in dashi-konbu
   wiped with a damp cloth
For the *ponzu* (citrus sauce)
   juice of 1 lime made up to 120ml/
   4fl oz/½ cup with lemon juice
   50ml/2fl oz/¼ cup rice vinegar
   120ml/4fl oz/½ cup shoyu
   20ml/4 tsp mirin
   4 × 6cm/1½ × 2½in dashi-konbu
   5g/⅛oz kezuri-bushi
For the *goma-dare* (sesame sauce)
   75g/3oz white sesame seeds
   10ml/2 tsp caster (superfine) sugar
   45ml/3 tbsp shoyu
   15ml/1 tbsp sake
   15ml/1 tbsp mirin
   90ml/6 tbsp second dashi stock, or
   the same amount of water and
   5ml/1 tsp dashi-no-moto
For the condiments
   5–6cm/2–2½in daikon, peeled
   2 dried chillies, seeded and sliced
   20 chives, finely snipped

1 Mix all the *ponzu* ingredients in a glass jar and leave overnight. Strain and keep the liquid in the jar.

2 Make the *goma-dare*. Gently roast the sesame seeds in a dry frying pan on a low heat until the seeds pop. Grind the sesame seeds to form a smooth paste. Add the sugar and grind, then add the other ingredients, mixing well. Pour 30ml/2 tbsp into each of four small bowls, and put the rest in a jug (pitcher) or bowl.

3 Prepare the condiments. Pierce the cut ends of the daikon deeply four or five times with a skewer, then insert pieces of chilli. Leave for 20 minutes, then finely grate the daikon into a sieve. Divide the pink daikon among four small bowls. Put the chives in another bowl.

4 Cut the meat into 1–2mm/¹⁄₁₆in thick slices, and place on a large serving plate. Arrange the vegetables and tofu on another large plate.

5 Fill a flameproof casserole three-quarters full of water and add the dashi-konbu. Bring everything to the table and heat the casserole.

6 Pour 45ml/3 tbsp *ponzu* into the grated daikon in each bowl, and add the chives to the bowls of *goma-dare*.

7 When the water comes to the boil, remove the konbu and reduce the heat to medium-low. Add a handful of each ingredient except the beef to the casserole.

8 Each guest picks up a slice of beef using chopsticks and holds it in the stock for 3–10 seconds. Dip the beef into one of the sauces and eat. Remove the vegetables and other ingredients as they cook, and eat with the dipping sauces. Skim the surface occasionally.

SLICED SEARED BEEF

JAPANESE CHEFS USE A COOKING TECHNIQUE CALLED TATAKI *TO COOK RARE STEAK. THEY NORMALLY USE A COAL FIRE AND SEAR A CHUNK OF BEEF ON LONG SKEWERS, THEN PLUNGE IT INTO COLD WATER TO STOP IT COOKING FURTHER. USE A WIRE MESH GRILL OVER THE HEAT SOURCE TO COOK THIS WAY.*

SERVES FOUR

INGREDIENTS
    500g/1¼lb chunk of beef thigh
        (a long, thin chunk looks better
        than a thick, round chunk)
    generous pinch of salt
    10ml/2 tsp vegetable oil
For the marinade
    200ml/7fl oz/scant 1 cup rice
        vinegar
    70ml/4½ tbsp sake
    135ml/4½fl oz/scant ⅔ cup shoyu
    15ml/1 tbsp caster
        (superfine) sugar
    1 garlic clove, thinly sliced
    1 small onion, thinly sliced
    sansho
For the garnish
    6 shiso leaves and shiso flowers
        (if available)
    about 15cm/6in Japanese or ordinary
        salad cucumber
    ½ lemon, thinly sliced
    1 garlic clove, finely grated (optional)

1 Mix the marinade ingredients in a small pan and warm through until the sugar has dissolved. Remove from the heat and leave to cool.

COOK'S TIPS
• If you don't have a mesh grill or griddle, heat 15ml/1 tbsp vegetable oil in a hot frying pan to sear the beef. Wash all the oil from the meat and wipe off any excess with a kitchen paper.
• If preparing this dish ahead of time, spear the beef rolls with a cocktail stick (toothpick) to secure.

2 Generously sprinkle the beef with the salt and rub well into the meat. Leave for 2–3 minutes, then rub the oil in evenly with your fingers.

3 Fill a large mixing bowl with plenty of cold water. Put a mesh grill tray over the heat on the top of the stove, or heat a griddle to a high temperature. Sear the beef, turning frequently until about 5mm/¼in of the flesh in from the surface is cooked. Try not to burn grid marks on the meat. Immediately plunge the meat into the bowl of cold water for a few seconds to stop it from cooking further.

4 Wipe the meat with kitchen paper or a dishtowel and immerse fully in the marinade for 1 day.

5 Next day, prepare the garnish. Chop the shiso leaves in half lengthways, then cut into very thin strips crossways. Slice the cucumber diagonally into 5mm/¼in thick oval shapes, then cut each oval into 5mm/¼in matchsticks. Scoop out the watery seed part first if using an ordinary salad cucumber.

6 Remove the meat from the marinade. Strain the remaining marinade through a sieve, reserving both the liquid and the marinated onion and garlic.

7 Using a sharp knife, cut the beef thinly into slices of about 5mm/¼in thick.

8 Heap the cucumber sticks on a large serving plate and put the marinated onion and garlic on top. Arrange the beef slices as you would *sashimi*, leaning alongside or on the bed of cucumber and other vegetables. You can also either make a fan shape with the beef slices, or, if the slices are large enough, you could roll them.

9 Fluff the shiso strips and put on top of the beef. Decorate with some shiso flowers, if using. Lightly sprinkle with the lemon rings, and serve with the reserved marinade in individual bowls.

10 To eat, take a few beef slices on to individual plates. Roll a slice with your choice of garnish, then dip it into the marinade. Add a little grated garlic, if you like.

PAN-FRIED PORK WITH GINGER SAUCE

REPUTEDLY CREATED BY A CANTEEN DINNER LADY AT A TOKYO UNIVERSITY DURING THE 1970s, THIS DISH, KNOWN AS BUTA-NIKU SHOGA YAKI, IS PARTICULARLY POPULAR WITH YOUNGSTERS.

SERVES FOUR

INGREDIENTS
  450g/1lb pork chops, boned
    and trimmed
  1 small onion, thinly sliced
    lengthways
  50g/2oz/¼ cup beansprouts
  50g/2oz mangetouts (snow peas),
    trimmed
  15ml/1 tbsp vegetable oil
  salt
For the marinade
  15ml/1 tbsp shoyu
  15ml/1 tbsp sake
  15ml/1 tbsp mirin
  4cm/1½in piece fresh root ginger,
    very finely grated,
    plus juice

1 Wrap the pork chops in clear film (plastic wrap) and freeze for 2 hours. Cut into 3mm/⅛in slices, then into 4cm/1½in wide strips.

2 To make the marinade, mix all the ingredients in a plastic container. Add the pork and marinate for 15 minutes.

3 Heat the oil in a heavy frying pan on a medium-high heat. Add the onion and fry for 3 minutes.

4 Take half of the pork slices out from the marinade and add to the frying pan. Transfer the meat to a plate when its colour changes; this will only take about 2–3 minutes. Repeat the process with the rest of the meat and reserve the marinade. Transfer all the cooked pork slices and onions to the plate.

5 Pour the reserved marinade into the pan and simmer until it has reduced by one-third. Add the beansprouts and mangetouts, then the pork and increase the heat to medium-high for 2 minutes.

6 Heap the beansprouts on individual serving plates and lean the meat, onions and mangetouts against them. Serve immediately.

DEEP-FRIED PORK FILLET

KNOWN AS TON-KATSU, SOME JAPANESE RESTAURANTS SERVE JUST THIS ONE INVIGORATING DISH. THE PORK IS ALWAYS SERVED WITH A HEAP OF VERY FINELY SHREDDED WHITE CABBAGE.

SERVES FOUR

INGREDIENTS
  1 white cabbage
  4 pork loin chops or cutlets, boned
  plain (all-purpose) flour, to dust
  vegetable oil, for deep-frying
  2 eggs, beaten
  50g/2oz/1 cup dried
    white breadcrumbs
  salt and ready-ground mixed pepper
  prepared English (hot) mustard,
    to garnish
  Japanese pickles, to serve
For the ton-katsu sauce
  60ml/4 tbsp Worcestershire sauce
  30ml/2 tbsp good-quality
    tomato ketchup
  5ml/1 tsp shoyu

1 Quarter the cabbage and remove the central core. Slice the wedges very finely with a vegetable slicer or a sharp knife.

2 Make a few deep cuts horizontally across the fat of the meat. This prevents the meat curling up while cooking. Rub a little salt and pepper into the meat and dust with the flour, then shake off any excess.

3 Heat the oil in a deep-fryer or a large pan to 180°C/350°F.

4 Dip the meat in the beaten eggs, then coat with breadcrumbs. Deep-fry two pieces at a time for 8–10 minutes, or until golden brown. Drain on a wire rack or on kitchen paper. Repeat until all the pieces of pork are deep-fried.

5 Heap the cabbage on four individual serving plates. Cut the pork crossways into 2cm/¾in thick strips and arrange them to your liking on the cabbage.

6 To make the ton-katsu sauce, mix the Worcestershire sauce, ketchup and shoyu in a jug (pitcher) or gravy boat. Serve the pork and cabbage immediately, with the sauce, mustard and Japanese pickles. Pickles can also be served in separate dishes, if you like.

SIMMERED BEEF SLICES AND VEGETABLES

THIS TRADITIONAL DISH, NIKU JYAGA, IS A TYPICAL HOME-COOKED MEAL AND IS ONE OF THE TRADITIONAL DISHES REFERRED TO AS "MOTHER'S SPECIALITY". IT IS A GOOD STANDBY, AS IT IS EASY TO COOK, AND THERE IS NO NEED TO BUY EXPENSIVE CUTS OF BEEF.

SERVES FOUR

INGREDIENTS
   250g/9oz beef fillet (or any cut),
      very thinly sliced
   1 large onion
   15ml/1 tbsp vegetable oil
   450g/1lb small potatoes, halved then
      soaked in water
   1 carrot, cut into 5mm/¼in rounds
   45ml/3 tbsp frozen peas, defrosted
      and blanched for 1 minute
For the seasonings
   30ml/2 tbsp caster (superfine) sugar
   75ml/5 tbsp shoyu
   15ml/1 tbsp mirin
   15ml/1 tbsp sake

1 Cut the thin beef slices into 2cm/¾in wide strips, and slice the onion lengthways into 5mm/¼in pieces.

2 Heat the vegetable oil in a pan and lightly fry the beef and onion slices. When the colour of the meat changes, drain the potatoes and add to the pan.

3 Once the potatoes are coated with the oil in the pan, add the carrot. Pour in just enough water to cover, then bring to the boil, skimming a few times.

4 Boil vigorously for 2 minutes, then move the potatoes to the bottom of the pan and gather all the other ingredients to sit on top of the potatoes. Reduce the heat to medium-low and add all the seasonings. Simmer for 20 minutes, partially covered, or until most of the liquid has evaporated.

5 Check if the potatoes are cooked. Add the peas and cook to heat through, then remove the pan from the heat. Serve the beef and vegetables immediately in four small serving bowls.

POT-COOKED DUCK AND GREEN VEGETABLES

PREPARE THE INGREDIENTS FOR THIS DISH, KAMO NABE, *BEFOREHAND, SO THAT THE COOKING CAN BE DONE AT THE TABLE. USE A HEAVY PAN OR FLAMEPROOF CASSEROLE WITH A PORTABLE STOVE.*

SERVES FOUR

INGREDIENTS

4 duck breast fillets, about 800g/
  1¾lb total weight
8 large shiitake mushrooms, stalks
  removed, a cross cut into each cap
2 leeks, trimmed and cut diagonally
  into 6cm/2½in lengths
½ hakusai, stalk part removed and
  cut into 5cm/2in squares
500g/1¼lb shungiku or mizuna, root
  part removed, cut in half crossways
For the stock
  raw bones from 1 chicken, washed
  1 egg shell
  200g/7oz/scant 1 cup short grain
    rice, washed and drained
  120ml/4fl oz/½ cup sake
  about 10ml/2 tsp coarse sea salt
For the sauce
  75ml/5 tbsp shoyu
  30ml/2 tbsp sake
  juice of 1 lime
  8 white peppercorns, roughly crushed
For the soup
  130g/4½oz Chinese egg noodles,
    cooked and loosened
  1 egg, beaten
  1 bunch of chives
  freshly ground white pepper

1 To make the stock, put the chicken bones into a pan three-quarters full of water. Bring to the boil and drain when it reaches boiling point. Wash the pan and the bones again, then return to the pan with the same amount of water. Add the egg shell and then bring to the boil. Simmer, uncovered, for 1 hour, skimming frequently. Remove the bones and egg shell. Add the rice, sake and salt, then simmer for 30 minutes. Remove from the heat and set aside.

2 Heat a heavy frying pan until just smoking. Remove from the heat for 1 minute, then add the duck breasts, skin-side down. Return to a medium heat and sear for 3–4 minutes, or until crisp. Turn over and sear the other side for 1 minute. Remove from the heat.

3 When cool, wipe the duck fat with kitchen paper and cut the breast and skin into 5mm/¼in thick slices. Arrange on a large serving plate with all the prepared vegetables.

4 Heat through all the ingredients for the sauce in a small pan and transfer to a small jug (pitcher) or bowl.

5 Prepare four dipping bowls, four serving bowls and chopsticks. At the table, bring the pan of soup stock to the boil, then reduce to medium-low. Add half of the shiitake and leeks. Wait for 5 minutes and put in half of the stalk part of the hakusai. Add half of the duck and cook for 1–2 minutes for rare or 5–8 minutes for well-done meat.

6 Each person prepares some duck and vegetables in a serving bowl and drizzles over a little sauce. Add the soft hakusai leaves, shungiku and mizuna to the stock as you eat, adjusting the heat as you go. When the stock is less than a quarter of the pot's volume, top up with 3 parts water to 1 part sake.

7 When the duck has been eaten, bring the reduced stock to the boil. Skim the oil from the surface, and reduce the heat to medium. Add the noodles, cook for 1–2 minutes and check the seasoning. Add more salt if required. Pour in the beaten egg and swirl in the stock. Cover, turn off the heat, then leave to stand for 1 minute. Decorate with the chopped chives and serve with ground pepper.

SUMO WRESTLER'S HOTPOT

THIS FILLING HOT-POT, CALLED CHANKO NABE, *IS PROBABLY RESPONSIBLE FOR THE VAST SIZE OF SUMO WRESTLERS, AS IT IS THEIR FIRST MEAL OF THE DAY AFTER 4–6 HOURS OF MORNING EXERCISE. YOU NEED A JAPANESE CLAY POT OR HEAVY PAN AND A PORTABLE TABLE STOVE OR A PLATE WARMER.*

SERVES FOUR TO SIX

INGREDIENTS
  2 abura-age
  1 bunch of shungiku or pak choi (bok choy), 200g/7oz, root part trimmed
  1 large leek, trimmed
  1 daikon, thickly peeled
  ½ hakusai
  1 dashi-konbu, 4 × 10cm/1½ × 4in
  350g/12oz chicken, boned and cut into large bitesize pieces
  12 shiitake mushrooms, stalks removed, a cross cut into each cap
  285g/10¼oz packet tofu block, drained and cut into 8 cubes
For the fish balls
  6 sardines, about 350g/12oz, cleaned and filleted
  2.5cm/1in fresh root ginger, chopped
  1 large (US extra large) egg
  25ml/1½ tbsp miso (any except hatcho or aka)
  20 chives, roughly chopped
  30ml/2 tbsp plain (all-purpose) flour
For the soup stock
  550ml/18fl oz/2½ cups sake
  550ml/18fl oz/2½ cups water
  60ml/4 tbsp shoyu
For the citrus pepper (optional)
  grated rind of 1 lime
  10–12 white peppercorns

1 Make the fish balls by chopping all the ingredients on a chopping board, or use a mortar and pestle to grind them. Alternatively, use a food processor. Pulse briefly so the texture is rough, not fine. Transfer to a container, cover with clear film (plastic wrap) until needed.

2 Blanch the abura-age in rapidly boiling water for 30 seconds. Drain under cold running water and squeeze out the water by hand. Cut each abura-age in half lengthways, and then quarter crossways to make eight rectangles. Cut each rectangle in half diagonally to make two triangles. You should have 32 triangles.

3 Cut the shungiku or pak-choi into 6cm/2½in lengths. Cut the leek diagonally in 2.5cm/1in thick oval shapes. Cut the daikon into 5mm/¼in rounds. Cut the hakusai leaves into strips crossways, keeping the leaves and stalks separate.

4 Grind the citrus pepper ingredients, if using, in a mortar using a pestle and set aside in a small bowl.

COOK'S TIP
At the end of the meal there is a tasty, rich soup left in the pot. Add 200g/7oz cooked udon noodles into the remaining soup and bring to the boil again. After 2 minutes, serve the noodles in bowls with plenty of soup and chopped chives on top.

5 Lay the dashi-konbu on the base of the pan. Pour in the ingredients for the soup stock to fill half the pan, and bring to the boil on a high heat.

6 To cook the fish balls, reduce the heat to medium. Scoop up the fish-ball paste with a spoon and shape roughly like a rugby ball using a palette knife (metal spatula). Drop into the boiling stock. Repeat until all the paste is used. Skim the surface of the stock frequently. Cook for 3 minutes.

7 Carefully add the chicken pieces, daikon rounds, the stalks of the hakusai, the shiitake and leek, then the tofu and abura-age. Simmer for about 12 minutes, or until the chicken is cooked. Add the soft parts of the hakusai and the shungiku and wait for 3 minutes. Remove from the heat.

8 Put the pan on the portable stove on the table, set at the lowest heat, or on a plate warmer. Serve small amounts of the ingredients in individual bowls. Guests help themselves from the pot. Sprinkle on citrus pepper, if you like.

DESSERTS
AND CAKES

Glutinous rice, azuki beans, squash, sweet potatoes and sugar

are, surprisingly, the most commonly used ingredients in Japanese

desserts; no dairy foods are used at all. It is not customary in

Japan to have a dessert after a meal, so the dishes here are

normally eaten as an accompaniment to Japanese tea.

GREEN TEA ICE CREAM

IN THE PAST, THE JAPANESE DID NOT FOLLOW A MEAL WITH DESSERT, APART FROM SOME FRUIT. THIS CUSTOM IS SLOWLY CHANGING AND NOW MANY JAPANESE RESTAURANTS OFFER LIGHT DESSERTS SUCH AS SORBET OR ICE CREAM. HERE, ICE CREAM IS FLAVOURED WITH MATCHA – THE FINEST GREEN POWDERED TEA USED IN THE TEA CEREMONY. IT GIVES THE ICE CREAM A SOPHISTICATED TWIST.

SERVES FOUR

INGREDIENTS

    500ml/17fl oz carton good-quality
      vanilla ice cream
    15ml/1 tbsp matcha
    15ml/1 tbsp lukewarm water from
      the kettle
    seeds from ¼ pomegranate (optional)

COOK'S TIPS
Sweet azuki beans and French sweet
chestnut purée can be used to make
other Japanese-style ice creams. Use
30ml/2 tbsp soft cooked sweet azuki
beans or 20ml/4 tsp chestnut purée per
100ml/3fl oz/scant ½ cup good-quality
vanilla ice cream.

1 Soften the ice cream by transferring it to the refrigerator for 20–30 minutes. Do not allow it to melt.

2 Mix the matcha powder and lukewarm water in a cup and stir well to make a smooth paste.

3 Put half the ice cream into a mixing bowl. Add the matcha liquid and mix thoroughly with a rubber spatula, then add the rest of the ice cream. You can stop mixing at the stage when the ice cream looks a marbled dark green and white, or continue mixing until the ice cream is a uniform pale green. Put the bowl into the freezer.

4 After 1 hour, the ice cream is ready to serve. Scoop into individual glass cups, and top with a few pomegranate seeds to decorate, if you like.

KABOCHA SQUASH CAKE

YOKAN (CAKE) IS A VERY SWEET DESSERT OFTEN MADE WITH AZUKI BEANS, TO BE EATEN AT TEA TIME WITH GREEN TEA. THE BITTERNESS OF THE GREEN TEA BALANCES THE SWEETNESS OF THE YOKAN. IN THIS VERSION, KABOCHA SQUASH IS USED INSTEAD OF AZUKI AND THE CAKE IS SERVED WITH FRUITS.

SERVES FOUR

INGREDIENTS
   1 × 350g/12oz kabocha squash
   30ml/2 tbsp plain
      (all-purpose) flour
   15ml/1 tbsp cornflour (cornstarch)
   10ml/2 tsp caster (superfine) sugar
   1.5ml/¼ tsp salt
   1.5ml/¼ tsp ground cinnamon
   25ml/1½ tbsp water
   2 egg yolks, beaten
To serve
   ½ nashi
   ½ kaki (optional)

1 Cut off the hard part from the top and bottom of the kabocha, then cut it into three to four wedges. Scoop out the seeds with a spoon. Cut into chunks.

2 Steam the kabocha for about 15 minutes over a medium heat. Check if a chopstick can be pushed into the centre easily. Remove from the heat and leave covered for 5 minutes.

3 Remove the skin from the kabocha. Mash the flesh and push it through a sieve using a wooden spoon, or use a food processor. Transfer the flesh to a mixing bowl, add the rest of the cake ingredients, and mix well.

4 Roll out the makisu sushi mat as you would if making a sushi roll. Wet some muslin (cheesecloth) or a dishtowel slightly with water and lay it on the mat. Spread the kabocha mixture evenly. Hold the nearest end and tightly roll up the makisu to the other end. Close both outer ends by rolling up or folding the muslin over.

5 Put the rolled kabocha in the makisu back into the steamer for 5 minutes. Remove from the heat and leave to set for 5 minutes.

6 Peel, trim and slice the nashi and kaki, if using, very thinly lengthways.

7 Open the makisu when the roll has cooled down. Cut the cake into 2.5cm/ 1in thick slices and serve cold on four small plates with the thinly sliced nashi and kaki, if using.

STEAMED CAKE WITH SWEET POTATOES

THIS SOFT STEAMED CAKE, KNOWN AS MUSHI-KASUTERA, IS NOT TOO SWEET, AND CAN BE EATEN LIKE BREAD. THE SECRET IS A LITTLE MISO, WHICH ADDS A SUBTLE SALTINESS TO THE CAKE.

SERVES FOUR

INGREDIENTS
200g/7oz/scant 2 cups plain (all-purpose) flour
140g/4¾oz/scant ¾ cup caster (superfine) sugar
45ml/3 tbsp sweetened condensed milk
4 eggs, beaten
40g/1½oz shiro miso
150g/5oz sweet potatoes
10ml/2 tsp cream of tartar
2.5ml/½ tsp bicarbonate of soda (baking soda)
30ml/2 tbsp melted butter

1 Sift the flour and the sugar together into a large mixing bowl. In a separate bowl, beat the condensed milk, eggs and shiro miso together to make a smooth cream. Add to the flour and mix well. Cover the bowl with clear film (plastic wrap) and leave to rest for 1 hour.

2 Trim the hard end of the sweet potatoes and thinly peel, then cut into 2cm/¾in dice. Cover with water. Drain just before using. Preheat the steamer, and line with muslin (cheesecloth).

3 Mix the cream of tartar and bicarbonate of soda with 15ml/1 tbsp water. Add to the cake mixture with the melted butter and two-thirds of the diced sweet potato. Pour the cake mixture into the steamer, then push the rest of the sweet potato on to the surface of the cake.

4 Steam the cake for 30 minutes, or until risen to a dome shape. Remove from the heat and cool a little. Serve warm or cold, cut into wedges.

STICKY RICE CAKE WRAPPED IN SWEET AZUKI BEAN PASTE

THIS TEA-TIME SNACK, OHAGI, IS AN ABSOLUTE FAVOURITE AMONG ALL AGES IN JAPAN. IT IS ALSO MADE ON OCCASIONS SUCH AS BIRTHDAYS AND FESTIVALS. DECORATE WITH CAMELLIA LEAVES.

MAKES TWELVE

INGREDIENTS
150g/5oz glutinous rice
50g/2oz Japanese short grain rice
410g/14¼oz can azuki beans (canned in water, with sugar and salt)
90g/3½oz/6½ tbsp caster (superfine) sugar
pinch of salt

1 Put the two kinds of rice into a sieve, wash well under running water, then drain. Leave for 1 hour to dry.

2 Tip the rice into a heavy cast-iron pan or flameproof casserole with a lid, and add 200ml/7fl oz/scant 1 cup water.

3 Cover and bring to the boil, then reduce the heat to low and simmer for 15 minutes, or until a slight crackling noise is heard from the pan. Remove from the heat and leave to stand for 5 minutes. Remove the lid, cover with a dishtowel and leave to cool.

4 Pour the contents of the azuki bean can into a pan and cook over a medium heat. Add the sugar a third at a time, mixing well after each addition. Reduce the heat to low and mash the beans using a potato masher. Add the salt and remove from the heat. The consistency should be of mashed potatoes. Heat it over a low heat to remove any excess liquid. Leave to cool.

5 Wet your hands. Shape the sticky rice into 12 golf-ball-size balls.

6 Dampen some muslin (cheesecloth) and lay it flat. Scoop 30ml/2 tbsp of azuki bean paste and spread in the centre of the muslin about 5mm/¼in thick. Put a rice ball in the middle, then wrap the ball up in the paste using the muslin. Open the cloth and gently remove the ball. Repeat the process until all the rice balls are used up. Serve at room temperature.

SWEET AZUKI BEAN PASTE JELLY

IN THIS SUMMERY DESSERT A DARK RED KANTEN AND SWEET BEAN CUBE IS CAPTURED IN A CLEAR
KANTEN JELLY, AND LOOKS LIKE A SMALL STONE TRAPPED IN A BLOCK OF MOUNTAIN ICE.

SERVES TWELVE

INGREDIENTS
200g/7oz can azuki beans
40g/1½oz/3 tbsp caster
(superfine) sugar
For the kanten jelly
2 × 5g/⅙oz sachets powdered kanten
100g/3¾oz/½ cup caster sugar
rind of ¼ orange in one piece

1 Drain the beans, then tip into a pan
over a medium heat. When steam
begins to rise, reduce the heat to low.

2 Add the sugar one-third at a time,
stirring constantly until the sugar has
dissolved and the moisture evaporated.
Remove from the heat.

3 Pour 450ml/¾ pint/scant 2 cups water
into a pan, and mix with one kanten
sachet. Stir until dissolved, then add
40g/1½oz of the sugar and the orange
rind. Bring to the boil and cook for
about 2 minutes, stirring constantly
until the sugar has all dissolved.
Remove from the heat and discard the
orange rind.

4 Transfer 250ml/8fl oz/1 cup of the
hot liquid into a 15 × 10cm/6 × 4in
container so that it fills only 1cm/½in.
Leave at room temperature to set.

5 Add the bean paste to the kanten
liquid in the pan, and mix well. Move
the pan on to a wet dishtowel and keep
stirring for 8 minutes.

6 Pour the bean and kanten liquid into
an 18 × 7.5 × 2cm/7 × 3 × ¾in
container and leave to set for 1 hour at
room temperature, then 1 hour in the
refrigerator. Turn upside down on to a
chopping board covered with kitchen
paper. Leave for 1 minute, then cut into
12 rectangular pieces.

7 Line 12 ramekins with clear film
(plastic wrap). With a fork, cut the set
kanten block into 12 squares. Put one
square in each ramekin, then place a
bean and kanten cube on top of each.

8 Pour 450ml/¾ pint/scant 2 cups water
into a pan and mix with the remaining
kanten sachet. Bring to the boil, add
the remaining sugar, then stir constantly
until dissolved. Boil for a further
2 minutes, and remove from the heat.
Place the pan on a wet dishtowel to
cool quickly and stir for 5 minutes, or
until the liquid starts to thicken.

9 Ladle the liquid into the ramekins to
cover the cubes. Twist the clear film at
the top. Leave to set in the refrigerator
for at least 1 hour. Carefully remove the
ramekins and clear film and serve cold
on serving plates.

SWEET PANCAKE

IN JAPAN, THE SWEET BEAN PASTE IS TRADITIONALLY SANDWICHED BETWEEN TWO PANCAKES TO RESEMBLE A LITTLE GONG, HENCE ITS NAME DORA YAKI; "DORA" MEANING A GONG. ALTERNATIVELY, THE PANCAKES CAN BE FOLDED TO MAKE A HALF GONG.

MAKES 6–8 DORA YAKI PANCAKES

INGREDIENTS
    65g/2½oz/5 tbsp caster
      (superfine) sugar
    3 large (US extra large) eggs, beaten
    15ml/1 tbsp maple syrup or
      golden (light corn) syrup
    185g/6½oz/1⅔ cups plain (all-
      purpose) flour, sifted
    5ml/1 tsp bicarbonate of soda
      (baking soda)
    150ml/¼ pint/⅔ cup water
    vegetable oil, for frying
For the sweet bean paste
    250g/9oz canned azuki beans
    40g/1½oz/3 tbsp caster sugar
    pinch of salt

1 To make the sweet bean paste, put the canned azuki beans and their liquid into a pan, then heat over a medium heat. Add the sugar gradually and stir the pan vigorously. Cook over a low heat until the liquid has almost evaporated and the beans have become mushy. Add the salt and remove from the heat. Stir for 1 minute, then leave to cool.

2 Mix the sugar, eggs and syrup in a mixing bowl. Blend well until the sugar has dissolved, then add the flour to make a smooth batter. Cover and leave for 20 minutes.

3 Mix together the bicarbonate of soda and water in a cup and then mix into the batter.

4 Heat a little oil in a small frying pan until very hot. Remove from the heat and wipe with kitchen paper. Return to a medium heat and ladle some batter into the centre. Make a small pancake about 13cm/5in in diameter and 5mm/¼in thick.

5 Cook for about 2–3 minutes on each side until both sides are golden brown. Reduce the heat if the outside burns before the inside is cooked. Make a further 11–15 pancakes.

COOK'S TIP
You can make a half "gong" by folding a pancake in the middle and filling the inside with a little of the bean paste.

6 Take one pancake and spread about 30ml/2 tbsp of the sweet bean paste in the middle leaving about 2.5cm/1in around the edge. Cover with another pancake. Place on a tray and repeat until all the pancakes are used. Serve the filled pancakes warm or cold.

GLOSSARY

A

Abura-age Fried thin rectangular blocks of tofu. Available frozen and fresh.
Aka miso A medium-strength flavoured dark red soya bean paste.
An Sweet bean paste.
Ankoh Monkfish or anglerfish.
Ao nori Green seaweed flakes.
Arame A brown variety of seaweed.
Atsu-age Thick, deep-fried tofu.
Awakuchi shoyu Pale soy sauce.
Azuki beans Small, brownish red beans, often used in sweet recipes.

B

Beni-shoga Salt-pickled finely shredded root ginger.
Biwa Loquat, a yellowish-orange fruit,

C

Cha-shu Pot-roast pork.

D

Daikon A long, white vegetable of the radish family.
Daikon-oroshi A fine-toothed grater especially intended for daikon.
Dashi-konbu Dried kelp seaweed.
Dashi-no-moto Freeze-dried stock granules for making dashi stock.
Dashi stock A stock for soups and hotpots using kezuri-bushi and konbu. It is possible to make your own dashi stock but stock granules (dashi-no-moto) are also available.

E

Ebi Prawns (shrimp).
Eda-mame Fresh, young, green beans in the pod.
Enokitake Small delicately flavoured mushrooms with slender stalks.

F

Fu Gluten cakes made from wheat flour, used mainly as a garnish.

G

Gammodoki Deep-fried tofu balls with vegetables.
Gari Thinly sliced and pickled ginger, available in packets or jars.
Ginnan Gingko nuts.
Gobo Burdock root, a long, stick-like root vegetable.
Goma Sesame seeds.

H

Hakusai Chinese cabbage, a crunchy vegetable with a white stem and green leaves.
Hamaguri Clams, available fresh, dried or cooked in cans.
Harusame Thin cellophane noodles made from azuki beans or starchy roots.
Hashi Chopsticks.
Hatcho miso Dark brown soya bean paste.
Hidara Dried cod fillets.
Hijiki Twiggy, black marine algae (seaweed) available dried.
Hirame A type of flounder.
Hiyamugi Thin white noodles, similar to udon.
Horenso Eastern spinach with thin leaves and a mild, sweet flavour.
Hotate-gai Scallops.

I

Ichigo Strawberries.
Ika Squid, available dried as a delicacy.
Ikura Salted orange-red salmon roe.
Ise-ebi Japanese spiny lobster with a brown or reddish purple shell.
Iwashi Sardines.

K

Kabocha A squash with dark green, ragged skin, rich yellow flesh and a nutty flavour.
Kabu Japanese turnip.
Kaki Japanese persimmon, similar to Sharon fruit.
Kaki Oysters.
Kamaboko Puréed white fish.
Kani Crab.
Kanpyo Dried gourd ribbons.
Kanten Agar-agar, a gelling agent made from seaweed.
Kashiwa Salted Japanese oak leaves.
Katsuo Skipjack tuna.
Katsuo-bushi Whole cooked and dried block of katsuo, ready for shaving.
Kazunoko Salted and dried herring ovaries.
Kezuri-bushi Ready shaved, dried katsuo flakes for dashi fish stock.
Kiku nori Dried chrysanthemum petals.
Kinako Yellow soya bean flour.
Konbu Giant kelp seaweed.
Konnyaku A dense, gelatinous cake made from the konnyaku plant.
Koya-dofu Freeze-dried tofu.
Kurama-ebi Tiger prawns.

M

Maguro Tuna.
Makisu Sushi rolling mat.
Matcha Powdered green tea.
Matsutake Large, dark brown fungus with a thick, meaty stem.
Menma Pickled bamboo shoots.
Mikan Satsuma or mandarin.
Mirin Sweet rice wine used for cooking.
Miso Mixture of fermented soya beans and grains that matures into a paste.
Mitsuba Aromatic herb used mostly for soups. Member of the parsley family.
Mizuna Japanese greens.
Mochi Rice cakes made from mochigome rice.
Mochigome Glutinous rice.

N
Naga-imo (or yama-imo) A mountain potato similar to a yam.
Nameko Slippery mushrooms (available only in jars or cans).
Nashi Russet-coloured Japanese pear.
Natto Fermented soya beans.
Negi Giant spring onion.
Niboshi Hard, dried sardines.
Nori Dried, paper-thin seaweed.

O
Oden Hot pot.
Okara Soya bean pulp.

P
Pak choi (bok choy) Loose-leafed brassica with white stems.

R
Rakkyo Bulb vegetable, often pickled. The Japanese equivalent of garlic.
Ramen Thin egg noodles made from wheat flour.
Renkon A white-fleshed root from the lotus plant.

S
Saba Chub mackerel.
Saikyo miso Pale yellow soya bean paste, lightly flavoured.
Sake A traditional rice wine for drinking and cooking.
Saké Salmon.
Samma Saury, a long, narrow fish.
Sansho Ground Japanese pepper with a minty aroma.
Sashimi Raw fish and shellfish sliced thinly and arranged decoratively.
Satoimo Oval-shaped potato, covered in a hairy skin.
Satsuma-imo Sweet potato.
Second dashi stock Stock made using reserved solids from first dashi stock.

Sencha Green tea made from the young leaves.
Shichimi togarashi Seven-spice powder, containing chilli, sesame, poppy, hemp, shiso, sansho and nori.
Shiitake A variety of fungus with a brown cap and white stem.
Shimeji Meaty-textured mushroom, similar to oyster mushrooms.
Shinjo Fish balls.
Shio-zuke Salt-pickled vegetables.
Shiratake Noodles made from konnyaku.
Shiro miso Pale yellow soya bean paste.
Shiso Basil-flavoured leaves.
Shoga Fresh ginger.
Shoyu Ordinary Japanese soy sauce.
Shungiku Edible leaves from the vegetable chrysanthemum.
Soba Dried buckwheat noodles.
Soba tsuyu Instant soya soup base.
Somen Very fine wheat noodles.
Sora mame Broad (fava) beans.
Sudachi Citrus fruit with firm, green skin and moist, yellow flesh.
Sukiyaki Wafer-thin meat and vegetables cooked in a sauce.
Su-meshi Vinegared rice.
Suribachi and **surikogi** A ceramic bowl with grooves inside and a pestle made of pepper wood.
Sushi Small rolls of *su-meshi* and flavourings topped with thin slices of raw fish.
Suzuki Sea bass.

T
Tai Sea bream.
Takanotsume Fresh red chilli.
Takenoko Fresh, young bamboo shoots.
Takuan Pickled and dyed daikon.
Tamari shoyu Naturally fermented dark soy sauce.
Tarako Cod ovaries.
Tazukuri Dried, small sardines.
Tempura A lumpy batter made with ice-cold water for deep-frying fish and sliced vegetables.
Tofu A nutritious, coagulated soya bean protein.
Tsukemono Pickled vegetables.
Tsuma Daikon cut into strands.
Tsumami Dishes to accompany drinks.

U
Udon Thick wheat noodles.
Ume Japanese apricot.

Umeboshi Salted pickled ume.
Uruchimai Short-grain rice.
Ushi-ebi Black tiger prawns (jumbo shrimp).
Usukuchi shoyu Reduced salt soy sauce.
Usu zukuri Very thin slices of fish.

W
Wakame A curly seaweed, available in a dried form.
Wasabi A pungent root similar to horseradish, available as a paste or powder.

Y
Yakitori Skewered grilled chicken.
Yuba Dried soya bean skin.
Yuzu A citrus fruit the size of a clementine with firm, yellow skin, inedible when fresh.

Shopping Information

United Kingdom
Arigato
48–50 Brewer Street
London
W1F 9TG
Tel: 020 7287 1722

Atari-Ya Foods
595 High Road
Finchley
London
N12 0DY
Tel: 020 8446 6669
www.atariya.co.uk

Atari-Ya Foods
7 Station Parade
West Acton
London
W3 0Ds
Tel: 020 8896 1552
www.atariya.co.uk

Hoo Hing
Bond Road,
off Western Road
Mitcham
Surrey
CR4 3FL
Tel: 020 8687 2633
www.hoohing.com

Japan Centre
19 Shaftesbury Avenue
London
W1D 7ED
Tel: 020 3405 1246
www.japancentre.com

SeeWoo
The Point
29 Saracen Street
Hamilton Hill
Glasgow
G22 5HT
Tel: 0845 078 8818
www.seewoo.com

T.K. Trading Japanese foods
Unit 6-7 The Chase Centre
Chase Road
Park Royal
London
NW10 6QD
Tel: 020 8453 1743
www.japan-foods.co.uk

Wing Tai Supermarket
Unit 11a The Aylesham Centre
Rye Lane
London
SE15 5EW
Tel: 020 7635 0714
www.wingtai.co.uk

Above: Two young Japanese girls enjoy baked satsuma-imo (sweet potatoes).

United States of America and Canada
99 Ranch Market
Tel: 1-800-600-8292
www.99ranch.com

Abestkitchen
424 West Exchange Street
Akron, OH 44302
Tel: (330) 535-2811
www.akitchen.com

Akasaka Japanese Restaurant
280 W Beaver Creek Rd
Richmond Hill, ON L4B 3Z1
Tel: (905) 764-9291
www.akasaka.ca

Asian Food Market
1011 Route 22 West
North Plainfield, NJ 07060
Tel: (908) 668-8382
www.asianfoodmarkets.com

Bowery Kitchen
460 West 16th Street
New York, NY 10011
Tel: (212) 376-4982
bowerykitchens.com

Daido Market
522 Mamaroneck Avenue
White Plains, NY 10605
Tel: (914) 683-6735
daidomarket.com

Fujiya Japanese Foods
912 Clark Drive, Vancouver, BC
Tel: (604) 251-3711
www.fujiya.ca

Left: A typically bustling Tokyo shopping arcade.

H-Mart
300 Chubb Avenue
Lyndhurst NJ 07071
www.hmart.com

Japan Super
www.japansuper.com

Japanese Style
Route 1, Box 301-B
New Prague, MN 56071
Tel: (877) 226 4387
www.japanesestyle.com

Katagiri
224 East 59th Street
New York, NY 10022
Tel: (212) 755-3566
katagiri.com

Minamoto Kitchoan
509 Madison Avenue
New York, NY 10022
Tel: (212) 489-3747
www.kitchoan.com

Mitsuwa Marketplace
100 E. Algonquin Road
Arlington Heights, IL 60005
Tel: (847) 956-6699
www.mitsuwa.com

Pacific Mercantile Co.
1925 Lawrence Street
Denver, CO 80202
Tel: (303) 295-0293
www.pacificeastwest.com

Sapporo Japanese Restaurant
96 Main Street E.
Hamilton, ON L8N 1G5
www.sapporohamilton.com

Sekisui
25 S Belvedere Blvd
Memphis, TN 38104
Tel: (901) 725-0005
www.sekisuiusa.com

Sunrise Asian Food Market
70 West 29th Avenue
Eugene, Oregon 97405
Tel: (541) 343-3295
see.org/sunrise
www.sunriseasianfood.com

T & T Supermarkets
www.tnt-supermarket.com

Tanto
839 White Plains Road
Scarsdale, NY 10583
Tel: (914) 725-9100
www.nytanto.com

Above: Japanese temple

Australia and New Zealand
Asian Food 4U
45 Plaza Parade
Maroochydore QLD 4558
Tel: (07) 5443 8109
www.buyasianfood.com.au

David Jones
86–108 Castlereagh Street
Sydney NSW 2000
Tel: (02) 9266 5544
www.davidjones.com.au

Ettason
2A Birmingham Avenue
Villawood NSW 2163
Tel: (02) 9728 2288
www.ettason.com

Exotic Asian Groceries
16 Surfers Avenue
Mermaid Beach QLD 4218
Tel: (07) 5572 0750
www.exoticgroceries.com.au

Tokyo Food
www.tokyofood.co.nz

Welcome Fresh Food
Shop 91, Sunnybank Plaza Cnr Mains Rd
& McCullough Street Sunnybank
Brisbane QLD 4109
Tel: (07) 3345 7688
www.welcomefreshfood.com.au

Left: Nebuta festival held in northern Japan each August.

INDEX

A

alcohol, 9
asparagus
  marinated and grilled
    swordfish, 98
  paper-wrapped and steamed
    red snapper, 95
aubergines
  fried aubergine with miso
    sauce, 50
  steamed aubergine with
    sesame sauce, 54
avocado, marinated salmon
  with, 81
azuki beans
  red rice wrapped in oak
    leaves, 22
  sticky rice cake wrapped in
    sweet azuki bean
    paste, 118
  sweet azuki bean paste
    jelly, 120
  sweet azuki bean soup with
    mochi rice cake, 68
  sweet pancake, 121

B

bacon-rolled enokitake
  mushrooms, 58
beansprouts
  salmon *teriyaki*, 88
  teppan taki, 99
beef
  paper-thin sliced beef
    cooked in stock, 105
  simmered beef slices and
    vegetables, 110
  sliced seared beef, 106
  sukiyaki, 104
beer, 9
black-eyed beans,
  cooked, 69
broad beans, daikon and
  salmon roe, 52
broccoli and cucumber
  pickled in miso, 64
buckwheat noodles with
  dipping sauce, 35
Buddhism, 7

C

cabbage
  deep-fried pork fillet, 108
cakes
  kabocha squash
    cake, 117
  steamed cake with sweet
    potatoes, 118

carrots
  carrot in sweet vinegar, 50
  daikon and carrot
    salad, 46
chicken
  chicken and egg on rice, 27
  five ingredients rice, 23
  grilled chicken balls cooked
    on bamboo skewers, 103
  grilled skewered
    chicken, 102
  hijiki seaweed and
    chicken, 59
  kabocha squash with
    chicken sauce, 49
  lunch-box rice with three
    toppings, 26
  New Year's soup, 33
  pot-cooked udon in miso
    soup, 37
  seafood, chicken and
    vegetable hot-pot, 94
  sumo wrestler's hot-pot, 112
chilli, and radish sauce, 99
China, 7
clams, and spring onions with
  miso and mustard sauce,
  92
cod
  lunch-box rice with three
    toppings, 26
crab
  clear soup with crab
    sticks, 31
  crab meat in vinegar, 90
cucumber
  broccoli and cucumber
    pickled in miso, 64
  wakame with prawns and
    cucumber in vinegar
    dressing, 62

D

daikon, 122
  broad beans, daikon and
    salmon roe, 52

daikon and carrot
  salad, 46
daikon layered with smoked
  salmon, 64
simmered squid and
  daikon, 88
slow-cooked daikon, 44
tempura seafood, 96
dashi, new potatoes cooked in
  dashi stock, 55
duck, pot-cooked with green
  vegetables, 111

E

eggplant *see* aubergine
eggs
  chicken and egg on
    rice, 27
  rolled omelette, 74
  savoury egg soup, 75
  thick-rolled sushi, 16–17
  udon noodles with egg broth
    and ginger, 36
enokitake
  bacon-rolled enokitake
    mushrooms, 58
  sukiyaki, 104

F

fish
  assorted fresh raw fish, 78
  see also salmon; tuna etc
five ingredients rice, 23
futo-maki, 16–17

G

ginger
  pan-fried pork with ginger
    sauce, 108
gingko nuts
  savoury egg soup, 75
green tea ice cream, 116

H

hijiki (seaweed) and
  chicken, 59

hishio, 6–7
hoso-maki, 16
hot-pots
  seafood, chicken and
    vegetable hot-pot, 94
  sumo wrestler's hot-pot, 112

I

ice cream, green tea, 116

J

jelly, sweet azuki bean
  paste, 120
jewel-box sushi, 14

K

kabocha (squash)
  kabocha squash
    cake, 117
  kabocha squash with
    chicken sauce, 49

L

lemon sole and fresh oyster
  salad, 80
lime and soy sauce, 99
lunch-box rice with three
  toppings, 26

M

mackerel
  marinated mackerel
    sushi, 12
  rice balls with four
    fillings, 20
  spicy fried mackerel, 85
mangetouts
  braised turnip with prawn
    and mangetout, 48
  salmon teriyaki, 88
mayonnaise, wasabi, 99
meat, 7–8
minimalism, 6
miso
  broccoli and cucumber
    pickled in miso, 64
  clams and spring onions
    with miso and mustard
    sauce, 92
  fried aubergine with miso
    sauce, 50
  miso soup, 30
  miso soup with pork and
    vegetables, 32
  pot-cooked udon in miso
    soup, 37
  Sapporo-style ramen
    noodles in miso soup, 39

mochi (rice cakes), sweet
    azuki bean soup with, 68
monkfish
    teppan taki, 99
mushrooms
    bacon-rolled enokitake
      mushrooms, 58
    brown rice and mushrooms
      in clear soup, 24
    deep-fried layered shiitake
      and scallops, 60
    deep-fried small prawns
      and corn, 93
    five ingredients rice, 23
    paper-thin sliced beef
      cooked in stock, 105
    slow-cooked shiitake with
      shoyu, 53
    sukiyaki, 104
    teppan taki, 99

N
Nanban, 7
New Year's soup, 33

noodles
    buckwheat noodles with
      dipping sauce, 35
    cold somen noodles, 38
    pot-cooked udon in miso
      soup, 37
    Sapporo-style ramen
      noodles in miso soup, 39
    soba noodles in hot soup
      with tempura, 34
    sukiyaki, 106
    Tokyo-style ramen noodles
      in soup, 40
    udon noodles with egg broth
      and ginger, 36
nori (seaweed)
    hand-rolled sushi, 15
    rice balls with four
      fillings, 20
    thick-rolled
      sushi, 16
    thin-rolled sushi, 16–17

O
oak leaves, red rice
    wrapped in, 22
okra
    tempura seafood, 96
omelettes
    rolled omelette, 74
    thick-rolled sushi, 16–17
oyster mushrooms
    five ingredients rice, 23
    paper-thin sliced beef
      cooked in stock, 105
oysters
    lemon sole and fresh oyster
      salad, 80

P
pancakes, sweet, 121
paper-wrapped and steamed
    red snapper, 95
peanut sauce, spinach with, 46
peppers
    crab meat in vinegar, 90
    teppan taki, 99
plum paste, rolled sardines
    with, 91
pork
    deep-fried pork fillet, 108
    miso soup with pork and
      vegetables, 32
    pan-fried pork with ginger
      sauce, 108
    Tokyo-style ramen noodles
      in soup, 40
potatoes, new, cooked in
    dashi stock, 55
prawns
    braised turnip with prawn
      and mangetout, 48
    deep-fried small prawns
      and corn, 93
    savoury egg soup, 75
    seafood salad with a fruity
      dressing, 82
    soba noodles in hot soup
      with tempura, 34
    tempura seafood, 96
    teppan taki, 99
    thick-rolled sushi, 16
    wakame with prawns and
      cucumber in vinegar
      dressing, 62

R
radishes
    radish and chilli
      sauce, 99
    see also daikon

ramen noodles
    Sapporo-style ramen
      noodles in miso soup, 39
    Tokyo-style ramen noodles
      in soup, 40
red snapper, paper-wrapped
    and steamed, 95
regions, 9
rice, 6
    brown rice and mushrooms
      in clear soup, 24
    chicken and egg on
      rice, 27
    compressed sushi with
      smoked salmon, 18
    five ingredients rice, 23
    hand-moulded sushi, 13
    hand-rolled sushi, 15
    jewel-box sushi, 14
    lunch-box rice with three
      toppings, 26
    marinated mackerel
      sushi, 12
    red rice wrapped in oak
      leaves, 22
    rice balls with four
      fillings, 20
    rice in green tea with
      salmon, 24
    sticky rice cake wrapped
      in sweet azuki bean
      paste, 118
    thick-rolled sushi, 16
    thin-rolled sushi, 16–17
rice cakes
    sweet azuki bean soup with
      mochi rice cake, 68
rice vinegars
    carrot in sweet
      vinegar, 50
    crab meat in vinegar, 90

S
sake, 7, 9
salads

assorted seaweed salad, 63
daikon and carrot
    salad, 46
lemon sole and fresh oyster
    salad, 80
seafood salad with a fruity
    dressing, 82
turbot sashimi salad with
    wasabi, 82
salmon
    broad beans, daikon and
      salmon roe, 52
    cooked black-eyed
      beans, 69
    marinated salmon with
      avocado, 81
    New Year's soup, 33
    rice balls with four
      fillings, 20
    rice in green tea with
      salmon, 24
    salmon *teriyaki*, 88
    seafood, chicken and
      vegetable hot-pot, 94
    see also smoked salmon
salt, 6
Sapporo-style ramen noodles
    in miso soup, 39
sardines
    rolled sardines with plum
      paste, 91
    sumo wrestler's
      hot-pot, 112
sashimi (raw seafood), 78
    cubed and marinated raw
      tuna, 84
    lemon sole and fresh oyster
      salad, 80
    scallops *sashimi* in mustard
      sauce, 86
    turbot *sashimi* salad with
      wasabi, 82
sauces, 6
    lime and soy, 99
    radish and chilli, 99
scallops
    deep-fried layered shiitake
      and scallops, 60
    scallops *sashimi* in
      mustard sauce, 86
    teppan taki, 99
sea bream
    seafood, chicken and
      vegetable hot-pot, 94
    seafood salad with a fruity
      dressing, 82
seafood
    hand-moulded sushi, 13

jewel-box sushi, 14
seafood, chicken and
    vegetable hot-pot, 94
seafood salad with a fruity
    dressing, 82
tempura seafood, 96
seasons, 9
seaweeds
    assorted seaweed salad, 63
    hand-rolled sushi, 15
    hijiki seaweed and
        chicken, 59
    rice balls with four
        fillings, 20
    thick-rolled sushi, 16
    thin-rolled sushi, 16–17
    wakame with prawns and
        cucumber in vinegar
        dressing, 62
sesame seeds
    lightly boiled spinach with
        toasted sesame seeds, 45
    rice balls with four
        fillings, 20
    steamed aubergine with
        sesame sauce, 54
shiitake (mushrooms)
    brown rice and mushrooms
        in clear soup, 24
    deep-fried layered shiitake
        and scallops, 60
    slow-cooked shiitake with
        shoyu, 53
    sukiyaki, 104
    teppan taki, 99
shoyu (soy sauce)
    lime and soy sauce, 99
    slow-cooked shiitake with
        shoyu, 53
shungiku
    paper-thin sliced beef
        cooked in stock, 105
    sukiyaki, 104
    sumo wrestler's
        hot-pot, 112
smoked mackerel
    rice balls with four
        fillings, 20
smoked salmon
    compressed sushi with
        smoked salmon, 18
    daikon layered with smoked
        salmon, 64
soba noodles, in hot soup
    with tempura, 34
sole, lemon, and fresh
    oyster salad, 80
somen noodles, cold, 38

soups, 29–40
    brown rice and mushrooms
        in clear soup, 24
    clear soup with crab
        sticks, 31
    miso soup, 30
    miso soup with pork and
        vegetables, 32
    New Year's soup, 33
    pot-cooked udon in
        miso soup, 37
    Sapporo-style ramen
        noodles in miso soup, 39
    savoury egg soup, 75
    soba noodles in hot soup
        with tempura, 34
    sweet azuki bean soup with
        mochi rice cake, 68
    Tokyo-style ramen noodles
        in soup, 40
    udon noodles with egg broth
        and ginger, 36
spinach
    lightly boiled spinach with
        toasted sesame seeds, 45
    spinach with peanut
        sauce, 46
sprats, deep-fried and
    marinated, 87
spring onions
    clams and spring onions
        with miso and mustard
        sauce, 92
    grilled skewered
        chicken, 102
squash
    kabocha squash cake, 117
    kabocha squash with
        chicken sauce, 49
squid
    simmered squid and
        daikon, 88
    tempura seafood, 96
su-meshi in tofu bags, 19
su-meshi rice, 12
sukiyaki, 104

sumo wrestler's hot-pot, 112
sushi, 8
    compressed sushi with
        smoked salmon, 18
    hand-moulded sushi, 13
    hand-rolled sushi, 15
    jewel-box sushi, 14
    marinated mackerel
        sushi, 12
    thick-rolled sushi, 16
    thin-rolled sushi, 16–17
sweet potatoes
    steamed cake with sweet
        potatoes, 118
sweetcorn
    deep-fried small prawns
        and corn, 93
swordfish, marinated and
    grilled, 98

T
tea, 7
    green tea ice cream, 116
    rice in green tea with
        salmon, 24
tea ceremony, 7–8
tempura, 7
    deep-fried small prawns and
        corn, 93
    soba noodles in hot soup
        with tempura, 34
    tempura seafood, 96
    vegetarian tempura, 56
teppan taki, 99
teriyaki, salmon, 88
tofu
    deep-fried tofu balls, 71
    grilled vegetable
        sticks, 73
    pan-fried tofu with
        caramelized sauce, 70
    paper-thin sliced beef
        cooked in stock, 105
    simmered tofu with
        vegetables, 72
    su-meshi in tofu bags, 19
    sukiyaki, 104
    sumo wrestler's
        hot-pot, 112
Tokyo, 8
Tokyo-style ramen noodles in
    soup, 40
tonkatsu, 8
tuna
    cubed and marinated
        raw tuna, 84
    hand-rolled sushi, 15
    thin-rolled sushi, 16–17

turbot sashimi salad with
    wasabi, 82
turnip, braised, with prawn
    and mangetout, 48

U
udon noodles
    pot-cooked udon in
        miso soup, 37
    udon noodles with egg broth
        and ginger, 36
umeboshi
    rice balls with four
        fillings, 20
    rolled sardines with plum
        paste, 91

V
vegetables
    grilled vegetable sticks, 73
    pot-cooked duck and green
        vegetables, 111
    seafood, chicken and
        vegetable hot-pot, 94
    simmered beef slices and
        vegetables, 110
    simmered tofu with
        vegetables, 72
    vegetarian tempura, 56
    see also daikon; turnips etc
vegetarian tempura, 56
vinegar
    carrot in sweet
        vinegar, 50
    crab meat in vinegar, 90

W
wakame (seaweed), with
    prawns and cucumber in
    vinegar dressing, 62
wasabi mayonnaise, 99
whiting
    tempura seafood, 96

Y
yakitori, 102